THE

ENEMY

UNMASKED

Second Edition

By

Bill Hughes

TRUTH TRIUMPHANT
Box 1417
Eustis, FL 32727
USA

THE ENEMY UNMASKED

TABLE OF CONTENTS

CHAPTER 1

DIVINE HAND OVER
THE UNITED STATES

The United States of America is at the brink of total collapse. Once a great and powerful nation, the United States is now in a free fall to disaster from which she will never recover. A few more steps in its decline and it will be ruined. These are not easy words for a patriotic American to read, but, nevertheless, they are absolutely true. Tragically, it need not have come to this.

As one looks at the history of nations, from Babylon to Rome to America, it becomes evident that a Divine hand was protecting and guiding America. From its humble beginning as a few colonies on the eastern seaboard it became the greatest of nations.

Alexis de Tocqueville, a young French philosopher of the last century, came to our shores to discover what magical quality enabled a handful of people to defeat the mighty British Empire twice in 35 years. He looked for the greatness of America in her fertile soil, her limitless forests and natural resources. He examined America's schools, her Congress and her unique Constitution without fully understanding the source of America's strength.

It was not, he said later, until he went to the churches of America and found congregations 'aflame with righteousness' that he began to comprehend the secret of this power. Upon his return to France, de Tocqueville wrote: "America is great because America is good, and if America ever ceases to be good, America will cease to be great." — Des Griffin, *Descent into Slavery?*, Emissary Publications, p. 267.

In her youth, the United States was very good. On her money, her trust in God was proclaimed, and the great blessing of God rested upon this nation. As the United States grew to greatness, she gradually abandoned the principles that made her great until today she is approaching a very tragic end. The process of the decline of America is similar to the decline and fall of the Roman Empire. Let us examine a little of the history of ancient Rome and notice the parallels.

As the early Roman Empire was beginning to develop, it was building on the solid premise that the family unit was the cornerstone of society. Morality and discipline were the cornerstones of the family unit. As the empire developed, liberalism crept in, and the morality and discipline that protected society began to disappear. By the beginning of the second century AD, most families followed the liberal trends, and their children were allowed to do pretty much as they pleased.

Having given up the habit of controlling their children, they let their children govern them, and took pleasure in bleeding themselves white to gratify the expensive whims of their offspring. The result was that they were succeeded by a generation of idlers and wastrels, who had grown accustomed to luxury and lost all sense of discipline. — Jerome Carcopino, *Daily Life in Ancient Rome*, Yale University Press, pp. 78,79.

As liberalism continued to progress, Rome eventually suffered "an epidemic of divorces." (ibid. p. 97) From the same author, we find that a strong women's rights movement developed in Roman society.

> Some [wives] evaded the duties of maternity for fear of losing their good looks, some took pride in being behind their husbands in no sphere of activity, and vied with them in tests of strength which their sex would seem to forbid: some were not content to live their lives by their husband's side, but carried on another life without him.... It is obvious that unhappy marriages must have been innumerable. — ibid. pp. 90,93,95.

Roman schools were in disarray.

> They undermined instead of strengthened the children's morals, they mishandled the children's bodies instead of developing them, and if they succeeded in furnishing their minds with a certain amount of information, they were not calculated to perform any loftier or nobler task.
>
> The pupils left school with the heavy luggage of a few practical and commonplace notions laboriously acquired and of so little value that in the fourth century Vegelius [A Roman writer who wrote about the Roman military system.] could not take for granted that new recruits for the army would be literate enough to keep the books for the corps. — ibid. pp. 106,107.

This kind of education led to a continual decline in morality and discipline and also resulted in decreasing patriotism.

> The Roman virtues — honesty, candor, frugality and patriotism — withered and died. What was left was a people whom neither the vices of the rulers nor the increasingly bold attacks of foreign enemies could shake out of their apathy.... In all the great cities of the provinces, the theater held the same place of bad preeminence in the social life of the inhabitants.
>
> The Roman stage was gross and immoral. It

was one of the main agencies to which must be
attributed the undermining of the originally sound
moral life of Roman society. So absorbed did the
people become in the indecent representations
on the stage, that they lost all thought and care for
the affairs of real life. — Philip Myers, *Rome: Its
Rise and Fall*, Ginn & Company, pp. 515, 516.

Another leading factor in the demise of Rome was
that it became a welfare country. People were encour-
aged to be idle and receive money from the government rather than work to make their own way. The welfare system was a

leading fact of Roman life. The evils that resulted
from this misdirected state charity can hardly be
overstated. Idleness and all its accompanying
vices were fostered to such a degree that we shall
probably not be wrong in enumerating the practice
as one of the chief causes of the demoralization of
society. — ibid. p. 523.

It is obvious that the moral fabric of America today
is where the morality of the Roman Empire was nearly
2,000 years ago. Do we not see the breakdown of the
home, a strong women's rights movement, a deteriora-
tion in the school system, moral decay as espoused by
the news and entertainment media, the schools, and
welfare eating the heart out of America? With regard to
these problems, how are we any different from the Roman Empire during its decay? Why are these things
happening in America? But, that's the wrong question.
The question should be: Who is orchestrating these
things to bring America to the brink of destruction?

As mentioned earlier, Providence had its eye on the
United States. America was the land of opportunity. It
was the place where those who were being persecuted
for their faith could come and worship God according

to the dictates of their own consciences. It was a land without a king where one could come and breathe the air of freedom. It was the place where one could come and earn a good living for himself and his family. America was the place where dreams came true. There once was a Divine Hand Over America.

In 1759, twenty-five years, more or less, stood between the thirteen colonies and freedom from the British. Twenty-five years and the world witnessed an unprecedented birth of freedom for the people. Twenty-five years and the framework for the Constitution — republicanism, inalienable rights, and a government of the people, by the people, and for the people — was in sight. The United States was an experiment in government that was never before tried in history, and it became the greatest nation the world had ever seen.

People have been taught for many years by the news media, the schools and colleges, and other means that the United States is a democracy. That is one gigantic lie. In the Pledge of Allegiance to the flag we see that the United States was set up to be a REPUBLIC.

> I pledge allegiance to the flag of the United States of America and to the REPUBLIC for which it stands, one nation, under God, indivisible, with Liberty and Justice for all.

. What is the difference? A democracy is a government where the majority rules, without exception, with no restrictions of any kind. A republic is a government based on law, where the law restricts the actions of government, and lists the things the government can and cannot do. The law that our republic is founded on is the Constitution. For instance, here is the first amendment to the Constitution:

> Congress shall make no law respecting an establishment of religion, or prohibiting the free exercise thereof; or abridging the freedom of speech,

or of the press, or the right of the people peaceably
to assemble, and to petition the Government for a
redress of grievances. — First Amendment to the
Constitution of the United States

It says that the government can make no law concerning religion. Even if the entire country voted to pass
a national Sunday law requiring everyone to go to
church on Sunday, it cannot pass because the Constitution forbids it.

An excellent example of a democracy is a lynch
mob. The majority wants to hang the guy, and the minority does not. So they have a vote and hang the guy.
There are no restrictions on a democracy.

Many said a republican government would not
work. The Roman Catholic Church had ruled the world
through the Dark Ages and sought to keep the world
under her dictatorial control. She was, and still is,
deathly afraid of such a government. For over 200 years,
the Protestant Reformation had challenged the papacy's
authority. The papacy gradually began losing her power.
A free country like America was certainly not in the
plans of the Catholic Church. The papacy could not allow a government to espouse principles that would bring
it down.

The monarchs of Europe ruled by permission of
the papacy and wielded tyrannical control over the
people for ages, with no one to oppose them. The papacy was not willing to permit the development of a
government where the people were free. Therefore, the
papacy coerced the nations of Europe in an attempt stop
this American experiment with every weapon at their
fingertips.

By the 1550s the Reformation had become so extensive in Europe that the papacy began to realize that
they must do something to try to stop it. They realized
that if it were not stopped, it would eventually undermine the position of the Catholic Church and destroy
the absolute political power they had achieved. In or-

der to accomplish the destruction of the Reformation, a new secret organization was formed within the Vatican, called the Jesuits.

One of the major purposes of the Jesuits is to destroy every trace of Protestantism and its principles, including religious freedom, republicanism, representative government, and an economy built around a strong middle class. Another purpose of the Jesuits is to greatly expand the power and control of the papacy throughout the entire world.

> I cannot too much impress upon the minds of my readers that the Jesuits, by their very calling, by the very essence of their institution, are bound to seek, by every means, right or wrong, *the destruction of Protestantism*. This is the condition of their existence, the duty they must fulfill, or cease to be Jesuits. Accordingly, we find them in this evil dilemma. Either the Jesuits fulfill the duties of their calling, or not. In the first instance, they must be considered as the bitterest enemies of the Protestant faith; in the second, as bad and unworthy priests; and in both cases, therefore, to be equally regarded with aversion and distrust. — G.B. Nicolini, *History of the Jesuits: Their Origin, Progress, Doctrine, and Design*, Henry G. Bohn, preface, [emphasis added].

> The first triumphs of the Reformation past, Rome summoned new forces, hoping to accomplish its destruction. At this time the order of the Jesuits was created; the most cruel, unscrupulous, and powerful of all the champions of popery…. There was no crime to great for them to commit, no deception too base for them to practice, no disguise to difficult for them to assume. Vowed to perpetual poverty and humility, it was their studied aim to secure wealth and power, to be *devoted to the overthrow of Protestantism*, and

the re-establishment of the papal supremacy. —
E.G. White, *The Great Controversy*, p. 234, [emphasis added].

From their very beginning in the 1540s, the Jesuits did just that. They used any means they could devise to destroy Protestantism, including assassination to kill leaders who tried to bring freedom to their people. Two examples are William of Orange in 1584 and Henry IV in 1610. Both were slain by Jesuit assassins.

The Jesuits used deception in the extreme to bring about the St. Bartholomew's Day Massacre in 1572, where 70,000 Protestant Huguenots, including women and children, were slain in one night. They also created the 30 Years War from 1618-1648 in order to destroy the Lutherans of Europe. The blood that reddened European soil for centuries can all be traced back to the murderous Jesuits.

Starting in the 1600s, the Jesuits created a communist regime in Paraguay that eventually brought the Jesuits demise in the 1700s.

> The Jesuits, as is well known, held very large regions of Paraguay under missionary control from 1650 to 1750. More than a quarter million natives worked under their direction, and no payment was made directly to them…. They were educated, trained, housed, clothed, fed and, to some extent, amused, but what became of the surplus profits of their labours, and of the extensive trading that was carried on? Over two thousand boats are said to have been engaged in carrying merchandise and goods on the Parana River; and the economic value of the Reductions [communes] was beyond doubt very great: so great indeed as to have awakened the envy of Spanish and Portuguese traders. Robertson [contemporary historian] estimated that the reductions represented at least $25,000,000 capital for the

Society. — Boyd Barrett, *The Jesuit Enigma*, New York: Boni & Liveright, p. 211.

The Reductions were communist communes set up as manufacturing facilities using the Guarani Indians as slave laborers. The products they produced were sold in Europe and greatly enriched the Jesuit order.

> The Reductions produced herbs, hides, tallow, clocks, and other goods, which the Jesuits traded in Europe with their huge fleet of ships. The profits were used to finance wars against the Protestant nations they had sworn to destroy. But all this wealth and power was acquired in secret, as the kings of Portugal and Spain knew nothing about the Reductions. — Eric Phelps, *Vatican Assassins*, Halycon Unified Services, p. 189.

By the middle of the 1700s, the Jesuit Order had become the powerhouse of Europe. According to Barrett,

> ...the Jesuit Order at last reached the pinnacle of its power and prestige in the early eighteenth century. It had become more influential and wealthier than any other organization in the world. It held a position in world affairs that no oath-bound group of men has ever held before or since...nearly all the Kings and Sovereigns of Europe had only Jesuits as directors of their consciences, so that the whole of Europe appeared to be governed by Jesuits only. — Boyd Barrett, *The Jesuit Enigma*, New York: Boni & Liveright, p. 209.

The Jesuits ruled the world. The monarchs of Europe, and the pope himself had Jesuits as their confessors. The plans and plots were all alike known to them. Besides this, they were amassing a vast amount of

wealth that allowed the Jesuits to do whatever they
chose. With them controlling the world, how could the
little colonies of America have had a chance to stand
against the Jesuit controlled monarchs of Europe? In
an instant, the Jesuits could utilize any army at its dis-
posal and crush the colonies. It was at this juncture in
1759 that something strangely divine began to happen.
It began in Portugal. The Portuguese king, Joseph I,
banished the Jesuits from his realm.

> In Portugal the culminating point was reached by
> an attempt to assassinate the king…the deed had
> been incited by the Jesuits, who had impressed
> ignorant and fanatical minds with the idea that no
> wrong was committed by killing a heretical king;
> *that is one who did not submit to their dictation*….
> Hence, as a measure absolutely essential to the
> life of the nation, the king issued a decree of
> banishment against the Jesuits as traitors, rebels,
> enemies to, and aggressors on, his person, his
> States, and the public peace and the general good
> of the people. The Jesuits were then seized,
> transported to the States of the Church (Italy)….
> — Richard Thompson, *The Footprints of the Jesu-
> its*, Hunt & Eaton, pp. 217, 218, (emphasis sup-
> plied).

King Joseph's Portugal was the first Catholic kingdom of Europe to banish the Jesuits from their realm.
With this first banishment, the dominoes began to fall
rather quickly. Catholic France banished them in 1762.
The decree of Louis XV and the French Parliament reads
as follows:

> Whereupon, the investigation into the consti-
> tution and statutes of the society [of Jesuits]
> …resulted in the enactment of a Parliamentary
> decree which shows the odium then attached to
> the society in France. It denounced their doctrines

and practices 'as perverse, destructive of every principle of religion, and even of probity; as injurious to morality, pernicious to civil society, seditious, dangerous to rights of the persons of the sovereigns; as fit to excite the greatest troubles in States, to form and maintain the most profound corruption in the hearts of men...that the institutions of the Jesuits should forever cease to exist throughout the whole extent of the kingdom.' — ibid. p. 219.

The third sovereign to drive the Jesuits form their realm was King Charles III of Spain. He banished the Jesuits in 1767.

His [Charles III] greatest work, the expulsion of the Jesuits, would never have been carried out if he had not been persuaded of its political necessity. The [Jesuit] order had already been driven out by Pombal from Portugal and by Choiseul from France when Charles III was convinced that a riot in Madrid...had been promoted by the Jesuits. — *Encyclopedia Britannica*, The Werner Company, vol. XVII, p. 341.

One year later, yet another nation banished this evil brood from their realm. Under the leadership of Fra Manuel Pinto de Fonseca, the Jesuits were forced to leave the island of Malta in 1768. Of this, we read:

In 1768 the Jesuits, having given much trouble, were expelled and their property confiscated. — ibid, vol. XV, p. 343.

The mightiest Catholic nations of Europe had banished the Jesuits from their realms. These Catholic monarchs demanded that the Catholic Church abolish the society forever. Clement XIII, the pope at that time,

resisted their wishes but finally capitulated. The night
before he planned to do this, he was poisoned to death.

> During the night preceding the day appointed
> for the public ceremony of announcing the aboli-
> tion of the Jesuits, Clement XIII was suddenly
> seized with convulsions and died, leaving the act
> unperformed, and the Jesuits victorious.
> Cormenin...records this event in the terse and
> expressive words: 'The Jesuits had poisoned
> him.'
> The Catholic Monarchies of Europe, how-
> ever, insisted that the Jesuits be disbanded and
> threatened the Pope.
> Clement XIII, after endless indecision, post-
> ponements, and unconvincing delays, finally de-
> cided to do what he had been advised he should
> do. He capitulated.
> He made ready a proclamation announcing
> the suppression of the Jesuit order. It was said
> that the document was written and was waiting for
> the day when it was to be made public. To the
> surprise of all, however, the Pope was suddenly
> attacked by a mysterious illness. He died on the
> 12th February (a coincidence in dates) 1769 with
> agonizing, unexplained convulsions.
> Rumours had it that he had been poisoned.
> The suddenness of his affliction and the convul-
> sions both pointed to it. The suspicions, however,
> were never proved. It was suggested by those in
> the know that the Pope had been made to die
> before he could publish the announcement of the
> official suppression of the Jesuit order. — Avro
> Manhattan, *Murder in the Vatican*, Ozark Books,
> p. 74.

Four years later in 1773, three years before the
Declaration of Independence, mark it well, Pope Clement XIV wrote an order, the purpose of which was to
abolish the Jesuits forever. (Unfortunately, a later pope
reestablished them in 1814.) Of this, we read:

Again, in July 1773, Pope Clement XIV wrote an order dissolving the Society of Jesus. This bull, *Dominus ac Redemptor*, was published 16th of August of that year. After issuing it, however, the Pope relented, in fear of the consequences, and tried to withdraw it. Too late. The Spanish ambassador had already dispatched the document by special courier direct to Madrid.

The papal brief annihilated the Jesuit order throughout the world, closed its schools and cancelled its statues. Its houses were occupied and its general and other dignitaries were imprisoned. — ibid, pp. 74,75.

In a 14-year period, from 1759-1773, the Catholic monarchs of Europe and the pope, himself, were preoccupied with abolishing the Jesuits. Emmett McLaughlin's tremendous book, *An Inquiry into the Assassination of Abraham Lincoln*, summarizes these events very succinctly with these words.

Even their own Catholic countries finally became surfeited with Jesuit political intrigue and financial avarice and, in self-preservation, were forced to expel them. Portugal, Angola, Goa, and Brazil took the lead in 1759. France followed in 1764. Several Italian states such as Parma, Sicily and Naples followed suit. By sealed imperial orders sent to her colonies around the world, Spain threw out all Jesuits in 1767. This decree suppressed them in the Philippines, Argentina, New Granada (Columbia), Peru, Chile, Ecuador, Guatemala, Cuba, Puerto Rico, Mexico, New Mexico and Arizona. Austria did the same in 1773.

Finally, Pope Clement XIV in 1773 issued the document, *Dominus ac Redemptor,* abolishing the Jesuit Order altogether, listing eleven popes that tried to curb their excesses. Among them were Benedict XIV, Innocent XI, Innocent XIII and Clement XIII. He cited the Jesuits for opposition to "other religious orders," for "revolts and intestine troubles in some of the Catholic states," and "persecutions against the church in Europe and Asia. There remained no other remedy to so great evils…and this step was necessary in order to prevent the Christians from rising one against the other and from massacring each other in the very bosom of our common mother, the holy church." Therefore, he wrote, "after a mature deliberation, we do out of our certain knowledge and the fullness of our apostolic power, suppress and abolish the said company."—Emmett McLaughlin, *An Inquiry into the Assassination of Abraham Lincoln*, Lyle Stuart, Inc., pp. 84, 85.

The timing of these events in Europe is fascinating. Catholic Europe was in disarray. The Catholic monarchs were preoccupied with taking care of the problems with the Jesuit Order. The Jesuits were reeling as one Catholic country after another drove them from their realms. While Europe was shaking, thirteen colonies across the Atlantic were looking at the very real possibility of war with England. The thirteen colonies were instituting principles of government never before heard in the annals of human history. Documents would soon be written that would codify such things as inalienable rights, government of the people, by the people, and for the people, free exercise of religion, and the right to keep and bear arms. These documents would soon be the hope of mankind throughout the world longing to be free.

What if the Catholic monarchs were not distracted by their dealings with the Jesuits? What if the Jesuits were not reeling by their banishment from Europe? The monarchs and the Jesuits would have utilized their wealth and military power to smash the American colonies in the New World, and the Protestant dream in America would have never been a reality. Without a doubt, there was a Divine Hand Over America!

Chapter 2

THE ILLUMINATI-JEWISH FRONT

There are many books and treatises on the conspiracy theory of history. It is very difficult to find any two of them that agree. Some say the perpetrators behind the scenes are the Illuminati, and others say the Jews. The list of the conspiratorial organizations blamed includes the Communists, the Bilderbergers, the Trilateral Commission, the Council on Foreign Relations, the Committee of 300, the Mafia, the Round Table, the Club of Rome, the Free Masons, the CIA-FBI-Mossad, and other secret societies. Of course the New World Order, the European Union, and the International Bankers must be included in this list also. Because of all the organizations accused of conspiracy, most people tend to disbelieve the conspiracy theory of history. If they do believe it, they tend to be thoroughly confused as to which organizations are responsible.

In addition to the organizations mentioned above, there are other conspiratorial organizations that remain in the background so that they are hidden from the view of the public. Let us investigate these secret organizations and discover the extent that they control our world.

Dr. Koryagina is the economic advisor to Russian president, Vladimir Putin. In a radio interview with Rick Wiles of American Freedom News, Dr. Koryagina declared:

> Everybody knows about organized crime and
> the Mafia. Also people have known for a long time

about secret societies and so forth. During my
research, I started to notice that *those structures
can be put together and joined. And I realized that
right now, we have a criminal monster, a hybrid of
organized crime, Mafia and secret societies that
have merged together.* (Aired Dec. 6, 2001)

This resulting gigantic organization takes its marching orders from one source, and has one human leader.
This chapter will show conclusively who the human
leader of the Illuminati, the Jews, and all these other
groups really is.

As we saw in chapter 1, the Catholic monarchs and
the pope, himself, were trying to ban the Jesuit Order
throughout the entire world in 1773. In order to sur-
vive, the Jesuits were forced to either go underground
or travel to three countries where they were still permitted to operate: England, Prussia (Germany), and
Russia. During this time frame, the Illuminati was created.

It is an unshakeable fact that the founder of
the modern Baverian Illuminati was a trained
Jesuit named Adam Weishaupt from Ingolstadt,
Bavaria. Weishaupt was a professor at Ingolstadt
University, which was the center of the Jesuit
counter-reformation. (See Encyclopedia Britanica,
Volume 12, page 251.) Ingolstadt was the center
where the Jesuits were flourishing in 1556. (See
History of Protestantism by Wylie, Volume 2, p.
413.)

Can we really believe that Weishaupt would
have been allowed to continue his professorship
in a Jesuit controlled University if he had deserted
them? No way! All evidence suggests that he
continued to work for the Jesuits, establishing the
order of the Illuminati for them. — Sydney Hunter,
Is Alberto for Real, Chick Publications, pp. 21,22.

On May 1,1776, the Order of the Illuminati was officially founded in the old Jesuit stronghold of Bavaria from which the Sons of Loyola had ignited the Thirty Years' War. — Eric Phelps, *Vatican Assassins*, Halycon Unified Services, p. 214.

From the Jesuit College at Ingolstadt is said to have issued the sect known as 'the Illuminati of Bavaria' founded by Adam Weishaupt; its nominal founder, however, seems to have played a subordinate though conspicuous role in the organization of this sect. — Lady Queensborough, *Occult Theocrasy*, Emissary Publication, p. 313.

The organization...is a secret society founded in Bavaria in 1776. Its founder, Adam Weishaupt, a professor of canon law at the University of Ingolstadt, labeled it the Illuminati Order. — Dee Zahner, *The Secret Side of History*, LTAA Communications Publishers, p. 26.

Canon law was the result of the infamous Council of Trent, which met from 1545-1563. This law revealed the Catholic Church's stand against the Protestant Reformation and is known as the Catholic Counter-Reformation. This council not only revealed the church's hostility toward the Reformation, but also how she would attack and destroy it.

Weishaupt established the Illuminati specifically to be a front organization behind which the Jesuits could hide. After being abolished by Clement XIV in 1773, the Jesuits used the Illuminati and other similar organizations to carry out their operations. Thus the front organizations would be blamed for the trouble caused by the Jesuits. Having so many front organizations would also confuse the people so that it would be virtually impossible to know who is actually manipulating the wars, policies, politics, and trouble caused by the Jesuits. The methods of many of these front organizations such as the Illuminati are carbon copies of the Jesuits' methods and techniques, which are still in use today.

> This passage exactly describes the methods laid down by Weishaupt for his 'Insinuating Brothers'—the necessity of proceeding with caution in the enlisting of adepts, of not revealing to the novice doctrines that might be likely to revolt him, of 'speaking sometimes in one way, sometimes in another, so that one's real purpose should remain impenetrable' to members of the inferior grades.
> How did these oriental methods penetrate to the Bavarian professor? According to certain writers, through the Jesuits. The fact that Weishaupt had been brought up by this Order has provided the enemies of the Jesuits with the argument that they were the secret inspirers of the Illuminati.... That Weishaupt did, however, draw to a certain extent on Jesuit methods of training is recognized even by Barruel, himself a Jesuit, who, quoting Mirabeau, says that Weishaupt 'admired above all those laws, that regime of the Jesuits, which, under one head, made men dispersed over the universe tend towards the same goal.... — Nesta Webster, *Secret Societies and Subversive Movements*, Emissary Publications, p. 197,198.

Thus far we have seen that Weishaupt was trained by the Jesuits, and the principles of the Jesuits were incorporated into the Illuminati in total. When Weishaupt created the Illuminati on May 1, 1776, he was teaching at Ingolstadt University, a Jesuit College. It is obvious that the Jesuits used Weishaupt to create the Illuminati as a front for their subversive activities.

> During the Order's suppression from 1773 to 1814 by Pope Clement XIV, General Ricci [the head of the Jesuits] created the Illuminati with his soldier, Adam Weishaupt, the Father of modern

Communism, who, with his Jacobins, conducted the French Revolution.... For the Sons of Loyola punished all their enemies including the Dominican priests, perfected the inner workings between themselves and Freemasonry, created an alliance between the House of Rothschild in establishing the Illuminati.... The Jesuit General was in control of Scottish Rite Freemasonry and now sought an alliance with the Masonic Baron of the House of Rothschild. To accomplish this he chose a Jesuit who was a German Gentile (not a Jew) by race and a Freemason by association-Adam Weishaupt.... Weishaupt established the Illuminati in 1776 and joined the Grand Orient Masonic Lodge in 1777. He united the magnificent financial empire of the Masonic Jewish House of Rothschild with the opulence of the international and secret, anti-Jewish Race, Gentile Society of Jesus. — Eric Phelps, *Vatican Assassins*, Halcyon Unified Services, pp. 206,205,213,215

The House of Rothschild financed Weishaupt in his creation of the Illuminati. Phelps alluded to this several times in the preceding quote. He is not alone in his assertion that the Jewish House of Rothschild worked hand in hand with the Jesuits in creating and funding the Illuminati.

After he [Weishaupt] formed his organization with financial backing from the House of Rothschild, he adopted the name Illuminati.... It was on May 1, 1776 that Adam Weishaupt backed and led by the House of Rothschild, formed the International Revolutionary force called the Illuminati, which later became known as Communism. — William Sutton, *The New Age Movement and The Illuminati 666*, Institute of Religious Knowledge, pp. 175, 231.

Aware that the Rothschilds are an important Jewish family, I looked them up in Encyclopedia

Judaica and discovered that they bear the title "Guardians of the Vatican Treasury...." The appointment of Rothschild gave the black papacy absolute financial privacy and secrecy. Who would ever search a family of orthodox Jews for the key to the wealth of the Roman Catholic Church? — F. Tupper Saussy, *Rulers of Evil*, Harper Collins Publishers, pp. 160, 161.

The expression "black papacy" is sometimes used to mean the Jesuits. The Jesuits are referred to in this quotation.

With the financial power of the Rothschilds behind Weishaupt's Illuminati, the Jesuits and the Catholic Church have an almost perfect cover to hide their operations from the view of the public. When investigators try to trace the roots of certain events, the Illuminati is a perfect shield behind which the Jesuits can hide, and behind which investigators cannot penetrate. The implications of this are enormous. We will briefly consider two items here but will examine them in greater detail in following chapters.

The book, *Descent into Slavery*, shows that there was a plan for both world wars and even a third world war.

This plan was outlined in graphic detail by Albert Pike, the sovereign Grand Commander of the Ancient and Accepted Scottish Rite of Freemasonry and the top Illuminist in America, in a letter to Giusseppe Mazzini dated August 15, 1871. [Knowing what we know about the Illuminati, Albert Pike was speaking as one who understood the Jesuits plan for world dominion to bring everything back into the pope's hands. Pike was the top Illuminist/Jesuit in America.] Pike stated that the First World War was to be fomented in order to destroy Czarist Russia-and to place that vast land under the direct control of Illuminati agents. Russia was then to be used as a 'bogey man' to further the aims of the Illuminati world-wide. [In other words, the Jesuits gained control of Russia near the end of WWI.]

World War II was to be fomented through manipulation of the differences that existed between the German Nationalists and the Political Zionists. This was to result in an expansion of Russian influence and the establishment of a state of Israel in Palestine. [In both instances, Pike's plan for world wars has been precisely carried out. These plans existed 40 to 60 years before the wars took place.]

The Third World War was planned to result from the differences stirred up by Illuminati agents between the Zionists and the Arabs. The conflict was planned to spread worldwide. — Des Griffin, *Descent Into Slavery*, Emissary Publications, pp. 38, 39.

Pike shows in that quote that the Jesuits are planning for a third world war between the Zionists and the Arabs. Zionists are those who are pro Israel like the United States and Great Britain. The so-called war on terror is part of the preparation for that war using Iraq, Iran, Al Qaeda, and others against the Zionists of America and Great Britain. The Jesuits are stirring up this conflict by their lies and deception, such as the false claim that Saddam Hussein was stockpiling weapons of mass destruction. This lie was simply a ploy to convince the American people that we had no choice but to invade Iraq. As will be shown later, the Bush administration is working closely with the Jesuits to carry out their policies to the letter. The current conflict was planned over 130 years ago!

The Illuminati/Jesuit connection also impacts us in another way. In Fritz Springmeier's book, *Bloodlines of the Illuminati*, we read that the two Bush Presidents were members of the Skull and Bones Order at Yale. The Skull and Bones Order is an entry point into the Illuminati. It is made to appear as just another exclusive fraternity, but in actuality a member of the Skull and Bones order is also a member of the Illuminati. We have seen that this means that the two Bush presidents are also members of the Jesuit Order and are carrying out their wishes. Springmeier also points out that the Bush family has been tied up with the Harriman family since the 1920s. The Harrimans have been intimately connected with the Skull and Bones Order/Illuminati/ Jesuits for decades. (See Fritz Springmeier, *Bloodlines of the Illuminati*, Ambassador House, pages 63, 320)

It is a most sobering thought to realize that the Jesuit Order controls the President of the United States. It is also a most sobering thought to think that this great Protestant nation is under the control of a man who is willingly carrying out the dictates of an Order whose stated objective is the destruction of every Protestant principle for which this nation stands. If permitted, this President would shred the Constitution. He is passing laws such as the USA Patriot Act and the Homeland Security Act, which totally ignore the restrictions on such laws in the Constitution.

This President has been told to engage in war in the Middle East. He has done so knowing that many lives of America's youth would be lost. This is nothing but a deliberate act of TREASON! When will Americans wake up and see what is being done to them?

Let us now examine the false claim that the Jews are really the bad people who are behind the scenes manipulating the world. Many people become very angry when this claim is made. The American Free Press, the John Birch Society, and others organizations of the media go to great lengths to slander and discredit those who believe the Jesuits are behind everything. Interestingly enough, the American Free Press invites cardinals from the Catholic Church to serve as their keynote speakers at meetings, and the president of the John Birch Society is a devout Roman Catholic. Is it possible that both the American Free Press and the John Birch Society, which both advocate a conspiratorial view of history, are actually being used by the Jesuits to sidetrack people from the real source from which all the conspiracies originate?

The propaganda in the media today tries desperately to convict the Jews as the real instigators of the trouble in the world. The Jewish belief that Christ will one day come and rule the world causes the Vatican to shudder. The Vatican believes that if hatred for the Jews can be fomented as took place in Hitler's Germany, then Jews will be ruthlessly eliminated. The Vatican believes that if all Jews are killed, Christ will not come, and the Vatican's aim to rule the world would remain intact. Avro Manhattan says it this way:

> It is important, although it may be difficult for some to recognize the religious nature of the Communist/Zionist/Catholic political configuration. Although deliberately muted in public pronouncements, behind the Zionist banner there was to be found the ancient Messianic hope for the coming of a global theocracy, as predicted by all the seers and prophets of Zion. It was to be a theocracy in which Jehovah, not Christ, was to be King.
>
> The spectre of the creation of such a theocracy has haunted the inner chambers of the Catholic church from her earliest inception, and still is a dominant fear.
>
> In Vatican eyes, therefore, the millenarian yearning for a global Hebrew theocracy, represents a deadly threat to the eschatological teachings of the Catholic church. When translated into concrete political terms, such a view spells not only rivalry, but implacable enmity. — Avro Manhattan, *The Vatican Moscow Washington Alliance*, Chick Publications, pp. 169, 170.

Why would the Jesuits use their implacable enemy, the Jews, to further their designs for world dominion? The Jesuits never do anything out in the open where they can be exposed. If they are recognized as the culprits, they will be blamed and suffer the consequences, but if they can use someone else as the cause of the world's problems, especially an enemy they can destroy in the process, then they have simultaneously accomplished two of their objectives. The Jewish people are the perfect scapegoat. Since the Rothschilds are Jesuits operating under a Jewish cover, using them in forming the Illuminati back in 1776 effectively throws the onus of this conspiracy on the Jews. The Rothschilds are certainly not the only Jesuits that operate under a Jewish front.

The following sources indicate that Adam Weishaupt and the Rothschilds were the brains and the wealth behind the French Revolution.

> History books will tell us that the French Revolution first began in 1787 or 1789, depending on which book you read. However, it was actually planned by Dr. Adam Weishaupt and the House of Rothschild almost 20 years before the Revolution took place. — William Sutton, *The New Age Movement and The Illuminati 666*, Institute of Religious Knowledge, pp. 172, 173.

> For the main purpose of Barruel's book is to show that not only had Illuminism and Grand Orient Masonry contributed largely to the French Revolution, but that three years after that first explosion they were still as active as ever. — Nesta Webster, *Secret Societies and Subversive Movements*, Emissary Publications, p. 255.

> They [the Jesuits] have so constantly mixed themselves up in court and state intrigues that they must, in justice, be reproached with striving after world dominion. They cost kings their lives, not on the scaffold, but by assassination, and equally hurtful as the society of Illuminati; they

were the foremost among the crowd, at all events, who applauded the murder scenes in Paris.... — Hector Macpherson, *The Jesuits in History*, Ozark Book Publishers, pp. 126,127.

The Jesuits, Weishaupt, and the Rothschilds managed to cast the blame for the French Revolution on their front organization, the Illuminati!

The Communistic ideals that came from the Reductions in Paraguay and that were exalted in France had their fruition in the writings of Karl Marx.

The ideas Lenin developed were directly from Karl Marx's Communist Manifesto, and ideas founded in the Communist Manifesto were directly from the writings of Dr. Adam Weishaupt, who took his orders from the House of Rothschild. — William Sutton, *The New Age Movement and The Illuminati 666*, Institute of Religious Knowledge, p. 193.

Karl Marx was hired by a mysterious group who called themselves 'The League of Just Men' to write the Communist Manifesto as demagogic boob-bait to appeal to the mob. In actual fact the Communist Manifesto was in circulation for many years before Marx' name was widely enough recognized to establish his authorship for this revolutionary handbook. All Karl Marx did was update and codify the very same revolutionary plans and principles set down seventy years earlier by Adam Weishaupt, the founder of the Order of the Illuminati in Bavaria. And, it is widely acknowledged by serious scholars of this subject that the League of the Just Men was simply an extension of the Illuminati... — Gary Allan, *None Dare Call It Conspiracy*, Concord Press, p. 25.

Karl Marx, 'the Father of Modern Communism...was privately tutored by Jesuits in the huge Reading Room of the British Museum while writing *The Communist Manifesto* based upon the ten maxims or 'planks' the Order had perfected on its Paraguayan Reductions.... A Jew was chosen for this task; for, the Order anticipated blaming all the evils of their Communist Inquisition on the Jewish Race. — Eric Phelps, *Vatican Assassins*, Halcyon Unified Services, p. 293.

Adam Weishaupt and the Rothschild family created the Illuminati. Then both Weishaupt and the Rothschilds united their efforts to control the French Revolution and the roots of Communism. The Jesuits next used Karl Marx to write the Communist Manifesto, which codified the Illuminati's plans. The teachings of Marx were then passed to Lenin, Stalin, and Trotsky. The financiers of all of these men were the Rothschilds or Rothschild agents such as Paul Warburg, the first chairman of the Federal Reserve Bank, Jacob Schiff and Armand Hammer. Each one of these men, being Jesuits were Jews and operated under a Jewish front. Is it any wonder that the Jews are usually blamed for all the conspiracies?

Other Jesuits who operate under a Jewish front include the former chairman of the Federal Reserve bank, Alan Greenspan, Senator Arlen Specter, and Henry Kissinger. The next chapter will further expose these Jesuit bankers.

Chapter 3

CRIMINAL BANKERS

Because Pope Clement XIV and the Catholic emperors across Europe were busy abolishing the Jesuits, they were not able to cooperate with each other well enough to stop the Protestant American experiment. If a Divine Hand had not intervened to protect the 13 colonies, there would never have been a United States with its God-given Constitution!

The Jesuits were greatly troubled because of their expulsions around the world, and they were forced to go underground. We have seen that they used their agent, Adam Weishaupt, to create the Illuminati and used the Jesuit House of Rothschild to finance it in order to create revolutions, and to destroy Protestantism around the world.

America was becoming a giant of financial affluence and prosperity, and was becoming a serious competitor for the Rothschilds and the papacy, who were trying to use their wealth to gain political and religious dominance in America.

> Aware that the Rothschilds are an important Jewish family, I looked them up in Encyclopedia Judaica and discovered that they bear the title 'Guardians of the Vatican Treasury.... The appointment of Rothschild gave the black papacy [Jesuits] absolute financial privacy and secrecy. Who would ever search a family of orthodox Jews for the key to the wealth of the Roman Catholic

31

Church? — F. Tupper Saussy, *Rulers of Evil*, Harper-Collins, pp. 160, 161.

The Jesuits used the powerful financial empire of the Rothschilds to obtain control through money and destroy America. Biographer Frederick Morton concluded that through the effective use of money the Rothschilds had successfully

> conquered the world more thoroughly, more cunningly, and much more lastingly than all the Ceasars before or all the Hitlers after them. — Frederic Morton, *The Rothschilds: A Family Portrait*, Atheneum, p. 14.

The Rothschilds believed that if they could control a nation's money, then they could control that country. This is clearly pointed out in the following statement from biographer Derek Wilson.

> The banking community had always consti-tuted a 'fifth estate' whose members were able, by their control of royal purse strings, to affect impor-tant events. But the house of Rothschild was immensely more powerful than any financial em-pire that had ever preceded it. It commanded vast wealth. It was international. It was independent. Royal governments were nervous of it because they could not control it. Popular governments hated it because it was not answerable to the people. — Derek Wilson, *Rothschild: The Wealth and Power of a Dynasty*, Charles Scribner's Sons, pp 79, 98, 99.

Using the vast wealth of the Rothschilds, the Jesu-its equipped armies to destroy countries that would not do what they dictated. They could buy politicians and through them change the very laws of a nation. This is exactly what they did in America and are still doing today! The Jesuits have used the Rothschild wealth to control major events behind the scenes worldwide for centuries. Today, however, they use the central banks in each country, including the Federal Reserve Bank in America, to supply them with funds. Central banks and how they operate are discussed in following paragraphs. To illustrate how the Jesuits and the Rothschilds have used countries and events to gain domination over nations and financial markets, we must look at the battle of Waterloo between France and England on June 19, 1815.

There were vast fortunes to be made, and lost, on the outcome of the Battle of Waterloo. The Stock Exchange in London was at fever pitch as traders awaited news of the outcome of this battle of the giants. If Britain lost, English consuls would plummet to unprecedented depths. If Britain was victorious, the value of the consul would leap to new dizzying heights.

As the two huge armies closed in for the battle to the death, Nathan Rothschild had his agents working feverishly on both sides of the line to gather the most accurate possible information as the battle proceeded. Additional Rothschild agents were on hand to carry the intelligence bulletins to a Rothschild command post strategically located nearby.

Late on the afternoon of June 19, 1815, a Rothschild representative jumped on board a specially chartered boat and headed out into the channel in a hurried dash for the English coast. In his possession was a top secret report from Rothschilds secret service agents on the progress of the crucial battle. This intelligence data would prove indispensable to Nathan in making some vital decisions.

The special agent was met at Folkstone the

following morning at dawn by Nathan Rothschild himself. After quickly scanning the highlights of the report Rothschild was on his way again, speeding towards London and the Stock Exchange.

Arriving at the Exchange amid frantic speculation on the outcome of the battle, Nathan took up his usual position beside the famous 'Rothschild Pillar'. Without a sign of emotion, without the slightest change of facial expression the stony-faced, flint eyed chief of the House of Rothschild gave a predetermined signal to his agents who were stationed nearby.

Rothschild agents immediately began to dump consuls on the market. As hundreds of thousands of dollars worth of consuls poured onto the market their value started to slide. Then they began to plummet.

Nathan continued to lean against 'his' pillar, emotionless, expressionless. He continued to sell, and sell and sell. Consuls kept on falling. Word began to sweep through the Stock Exchange: 'Rothschild knows.' 'Rothschild knows.' 'Wellington has lost at Waterloo.'

The selling turned into a panic as people rushed to unload their 'worthless' consuls or paper money for gold and silver in the hope of retaining at least part of their wealth. Consuls continued their nosedive towards oblivion. After several hours of feverish trading the consul lay in ruins. It was selling for about five cents on the dollar.

Nathan Rothschild, emotionless and expressionless as ever, still leaned against his pillar. He continued to give subtle signals. But these signals were different. They were so subtly different that only the highly trained Rothschild agents could detect the change. On the cue from their boss dozens of Rothschild agents made their way to the order desks around the Exchange and bought every consul in sight for just a 'song'.

A short time later the 'official' news arrived in the British capital. England was now the master of the European scene.

Within seconds the consul skyrocketed to above its original value. As the significance of the British victory began to sink into the public consciousness, the value of the consuls rose ever higher.

Napoleon had 'met his Waterloo.' Nathan had bought control of the British economy. Overnight his already vast fortune was multiplied twenty times over. — Des Griffin, *Descent Into Slavery*, Emissary Publications, pp. 27, 28.

By 1815, the Jesuits had complete control over England. If a leader did not do as he was told, money would be used to kill, smear, destroy, blackmail, or just drive the person from office. Later chapters will show that this procedure is being used today to control people like George Bush and Tony Blair. What was done in England is being done in many countries today.

As the new nation of America began to spread its wings, it would need a sound financial base from which to operate. It needed a bank, all right, but the bank used America instead of America using the bank. Financial genius and opportunist, Robert Morris organized the first central bank. He and his associates believed that the bank should be modeled after the Bank of England. While the first bank in North America was not as ruthless as the central banks of today, it performed many of the operations of a modern central bank. "Secret" investors put up $400,000 to start this bank. This bank lasted for two years. We will identify the "secret investors" in following paragraphs.

Please understand that the central banks being established by the Jesuits and the Rothschilds are in no way similar to the neighborhood banks that we all use to manage our money. Let us take a closer look at the central bank and see why it is so dangerous. We will use the Federal Reserve Bank as an example. Here is a very simplified scenario that pretty much explains one of the operations of the Federal Reserve Bank.

It is necessary to understand that the Federal Reserve Bank is not owned by the United States government as many believe. The central bank, the Federal Reserve Bank, is a private bank, owned by some of the richest and most powerful people in the world. This bank has nothing to do with the U.S. government other than the connection, which allows the operation described below. The private Federal Reserve Bank has a total, government-enforced monopoly in money. Before we had the central bank, each individual bank competed with other banks; the customers, the consumers, got the best deal. Not any more.

We all know that today the United States government borrows money and operates under astronomical debt. Why is this? Common sense dictates that a policy of such enormous debt will sooner or later destroy the organization that practices it, because the interest on its debt must increase beyond its income, making payoff impossible.

Now to our scenario. Here, roughly, is how the operation proceeds. Suppose the United States government wants to borrow a billion dollars. The government issues a bond for this amount, much as a water company does when it wants to raise money for a new pipeline or a new dam. The government delivers this bond for the billion dollars to the Federal Reserve Bank. The Federal Reserve Bank takes the bond and writes an order to the Department of Printing and Engraving to print the billion dollars' worth of bills. After about two weeks or so, when the bills are printed, the Department of Printing and Engraving ships the bills to the Federal Reserve Bank, which then writes a check for about two thousand dollars to pay for printing the billion dollars' worth of bills. The Federal Reserve Bank then takes the billion dollars and lends the billion dollars to the United States government, and the people of the country pay interest at an exorbitant rate each year on this money, which came out of nothing. The owners of the Federal Reserve Bank put up nothing for this money.

We see, therefore, that when the United States government goes into debt one dollar, a dollar plus the interest goes into the pockets of the owners of the Federal Reserve Bank. This is the largest, the most colossal theft ever perpetrated in the history of mankind, and it is so slick, so subtle, and so obfuscated by propaganda from the news media that the victims are not even aware of what is happening. You can see why the Jesuits want to keep this operation secret.

The Constitution of the United States gives to Congress the power to coin money. If Congress coined its own money as the Constitution directs, it would not have to pay the hundreds of billions of dollars of interest that it now pays each year to the bankers for the national debt, for money that came out of nothing. Money coined by Congress would be debt free. All the central banks in other countries operate the way the Federal Reserve does.

Secretary of the Treasury, Alexander Hamilton, submitted a proposal to Congress in 1790 for a central bank. Interestingly enough, Hamilton had been an aide of Robert Morris in the initial experience of central banking in North America. Surprisingly, during the Constitutional Convention of 1787, Hamilton had been a strong supporter of sound money. That Hamilton completely shifted his position within three years and proposed a central bank, which could generate the phony money as the Federal Reserve Bank does, shows that Hamilton's loyalty was completely compromised by the Jesuits. Notice the title of the book this next quote is taken from. The Creature from Jekyll Island is the Federal Reserve Bank. This bank was planned by conspirators who met for this purpose on Jekyll Island.

> This is hard to reconcile, and one must suspect that, even the most well intentioned of men can become corrupted by the temptations of wealth and power. — G. Edward Griffin, *The Creature from Jekyll Island*, American Opinion, p. 328.

Note carefully Griffin's conclusion. For Alexander Hamilton to have shifted so drastically within a few short years would lead us to believe that he had been bribed or blackmailed by the "secret investors."

Thomas Jefferson clearly saw what a central bank would do to America, and he gave the following most profound warning:

> A private central bank issuing the public currency is a greater menace to the liberties of the people than a standing army. — *The Writings of Thomas Jefferson*, Volume X, G. P. Putnam & Sons, page 31.

Jefferson realized that if a central bank was ever set up in America, the bankers would have virtually unlimited amounts of money to control how lawmakers voted, and to control the media and what they said. Within a short time, these bankers would essentially rewrite the Constitution and the Bill of Rights by the unconstitutional laws that they would pass. Thomas Jefferson was completely correct, for today we have enough unconstitutional laws, such as the USA Patriotic Act and the Homeland Security Act, to literally convert the United States into a police state after all the provisions of these acts are implemented.

Just like the old Bank of North America, the new Bank of the United States had eighty percent of its initial funding capital provided by "secret investors," and the government put up only twenty percent. Whoever these "secret investors" were, they had tremendous power in America because they had control of the money in America. Many books written about that time period tell us who these people were.

> Under the surface, the Rothschilds long had a powerful influence in dictating American financial laws. The law records show that *they were the power in the old Bank of the United States.* — Gustavus Myers, *History of the Great American Fortunes*, Random House, p. 556 [emphasis added].

> Over the years since N. M. [Nathan Rothschild], the Manchester textile manufacturer, had bought cotton from the Southern states, Rothschilds had developed heavy American commitments. Nathan...had made loans to various states of the Union, had been, for a time, the official European banker for the US government and was a pledged supporter of the Bank of the United States. — Derek Wilson, *Rothschild: The Wealth and Power of a Dynasty*, Charles Scribner's Sons, p. 178.

The Rothschilds and the Jesuits have been using their vast wealth to take over the United States through their traitorous politicians for a great many years.

During the time of the Rothschilds in Victorian England, Benjamin Disraeli was the Prime Minister for many years. In 1844, he wrote a political novel entitled Coningsby. One of the key characters in the book was a very powerful merchant and banker by the name of Sidonia. It is apparent from the events chronicled, that Sidonia is really Nathan Rothschild of England. In the book, Disraeli declares,

> Europe did require money, and Sidonia [Nathan Rothschild] was ready to lend it to Europe. France wanted some; Austria more; Prussia a little; Russia a few millions. Sidonia could furnish them all.

It is not difficult to conceive that, after having pursued the career we have intimated for about ten years, Sidonia [Nathan Rothschild] had become one of the most considerable personages in Europe. He had established a brother, or a near relative, in whom he could confide, in most of the principal capitals. *He was lord and master of the money market of the world, and of course virtually lord and master of everything else. He literally held the revenues of Southern Italy in pawn; and monarchs and ministers of all countries courted his advice and were guided by his suggestions.* — Benjamin Disraeli, *Coningsby*, Alfred A. Knopf, p. 225 [emphasis added].

The Jesuits and the Rothschilds would settle for nothing less.

After the Hamilton Central Bank failed, the Jesuits were able to establish a third central bank using Nicholas Biddle as their agent in 1816. The charter for this bank ran until 1836. Biddle made an attempt to renew the charter of this third bank during the Presidential campaign of 1832. Biddle believed that Andrew Jackson would not dare to risk his second term in office by opposing him, so Biddle felt this was the perfect time to renew the bank's charter. Andrew Jackson understood the dangers of the central bank and vetoed the bill to renew the bank's charter. Jackson's argument was simple.

Is there no danger to our liberty and independence in a bank that in its nature has so little to bind it to our country?...[Is there not] cause to tremble for the purity of our elections in peace and for the independence of our country in war?... Of the course which would be pursued by a bank almost wholly owned by the subjects of a foreign power, and managed by those whose interests, if not affections, would run in the same direction there can be no doubt... Controlling our currency,

receiving our public monies, and holding thousands of our citizens in dependence, it would be
more formidable and dangerous than a naval and
military power of the enemy. — Herman E. Krooss,
*Documentary History of Banking and Currency in
the United States*, Chelsea House, pp. 26, 27.

Jackson feared that the foreigners, who wanted to
dominate and control America, would use the central
bank to destroy her. The Rothschilds and the Jesuits
have been doing just that for many years using the Federal Reserve Bank. The following quote shows how
Nicholas Biddle manipulated the Congress.

Biddle had one powerful advantage over his
adversary. For all practical purposes, Congress
was in his pocket. Or, more accurately, the prod-
uct of his generosity was in the pockets of Congressmen. Following the Rothschild Formula,
Biddle had been careful to reward compliant politicians with success in the business world. Few of
them would bite the hand that fed them. Even the
great Senator, Daniel Webster, found himself
kneeling at Biddle's throne. — G. Edward Griffin,
The Creature from Jekyll Island, American Opinion, p. 351.

By the early 1830s the Biddle/Rothschild/Jesuit
plan was working perfectly. They controlled the congressmen and senators of the United States by giving
them money to become successful in the business world.
As long as the congressmen voted as they were told,
their businesses did well, but if they disobeyed the bankers, their money and other resources were withheld, and
their businesses failed.

Biddle was not without resources. In keeping
with his belief that banking was the ultimate source
of power, he had regularly advanced funds to

members of Congress when delay on appropriations bills had held up their pay. Daniel Webster was, at various times, a director of the Bank and on retainer as its counsel. "I believe my retainer has not been renewed or refreshed as usual. If it be wished that my relation to the Bank be continued, it may be well to send me the usual retainers." Numerous other men of distinction had been accommodated, including members of the press.
— John Kenneth Galbraith, *Money: Whence It Came, Where It Went*, Houghton Mifflin, page 80.

Webster's record in Congress had previously been in behalf of sound money. When Biddle bought Webster with money and other enticements, he succumbed and became a supporter of the corrupt banking objectives of Biddle. Webster became one of the central bank's most avid supporters. How tragic that Daniel Webster did not have the moral courage to withstand Biddle's bribes. In the early 1830s Congress had many Jesuits seeking to secretly undermine the great principles of our Constitution.

When Andrew Jackson finally ousted Nicholas Biddle and the central bank, he had to face other things such as Jesuit assassins.

With these accomplishments close on the heels of his victory over the Bank, the President had earned the undying hatred of monetary scientists, both in America and abroad. It is not surprising, therefore, that on January 30, 1835, an assassination attempt was made against him. Miraculously, both pistols of the assailant misfired, and Jackson was spared by a quirk of fate. It was the first such attempt to be made against the life of a President of the United States. The would-be assassin was Richard Lawrence who either was truly insane or who pretended to be insane to escape harsh punishment. At any rate, Lawrence was found not guilty due to insanity. Later, he

boasted to friends that he had been in touch with
powerful people in Europe who had promised to
protect him from punishment should he be caught.
— G. Edward Griffin, *The Creature from Jekyll
Island*, American Opinion, p. 357.

The Rothschild-Jesuit conspirators are ruthless, sick
individuals who will stop at nothing until Protestantism and the United States are destroyed, and the papacy rules the world again.

The Rothschilds and the Jesuits needed to regroup.
For the next 20 years, the name of the game was assassination as two presidents were poisoned and one was
almost killed by poisoning. Then the Civil War began
in America. According to German Chancellor, Otto von
Bismarck, all this, including the Civil War, was carefully planned.

The division of the United States into federa-
tions of equal force was decided long before the
Civil War by the high financial powers of Europe.
These bankers were afraid that the United States,
if they remained in one block and as one nation,
would attain economic and financial independence, which would upset their financial domination over the Europe and the world. Of course, in
the 'inner circle' of Finance, the voice of the
Rothschilds prevailed. They saw an opportunity
for prodigious booty if they could substitute two
feeble democracies, burdened with debt to the
financiers,...in place of a vigorous Republic suffi-
cient unto herself. Therefore, they sent their em-
issaries into the field to exploit the question of
slavery and to drive a wedge between the two
parts of the Union... The rupture between the
North and the South became inevitable; the masters of European finance employed all their forces
to bring it about and to turn it their advantage. —
G. Edward Griffin, *The Creature from Jekyll Island*, American Opinion, p. 374.

The Rothschilds and Jesuits used the Civil War to divide the United States into two contending countries. This would make America weak and much easier to control. It would facilitate America becoming enslaved to the Jesuits of Rome. In spite of the fact that the Civil War failed to accomplish the destruction of the United States, the Jesuits achieved much of their goal anyway, as conditions in the United States plainly show today.

President Lincoln understood the insidious hand of the Rothschild and Jesuit schemers in the Civil War. He understood the massive destructive power of these people. He knew that they were relentless in their pursuit of the destruction of the United States. Lincoln greatly feared for the survival of America and did everything he could to defeat their purposes. He said,

> The money power [the Rothschilds and the Jesuits] preys upon the nation in times of peace and conspires against it in times of adversity. It is more despotic than monarchy, more insolent than autocracy, more selfish than bureaucracy. I see in the near future a crisis approaching that unnerves me and causes me to tremble for the safety of my country. Corporations have been enthroned, an era of corruption will follow, and the money power of the country will endeavor to prolong its reign by working upon the prejudices of the people, until the wealth is aggregated in a few hands, and the republic is destroyed. — Archer Shaw, ed., *The Lincoln Encyclopedia: The Spoken and Written Words of A. Lincoln*, Macmillan, p. 40.

How prophetic; that is exactly what has happened. Abraham Lincoln saw that the Rothschild-Jesuit scheme was compromising the leaders of America. By utilizing their endless supplies of money, these evil men controlled many political leaders at the highest levels of the American government, and that was in the mid 1800s. Today the situation is much worse. American

politicians, members of congress, and government officials are selling their country to the Jesuits for the
chance to be wealthy and influential. We saw that even
the great Daniel Webster was a pawn in their hands. In
a speech in 1837, Lincoln declared,

> No foreign power or combination of foreign
> powers could by force take a drink from the Ohio
> or make a track on the Blue Ridge. At what point,
> then, is the approach of danger to be expected? If
> it ever reaches us, it must spring from among us,
> it cannot come from abroad. If destruction be our
> lot, we must ourselves be its author and finisher.
> As a nation of freedom, we must live through all
> time or die of suicide. — Joan Veon, *The United
> Nations' Global Straightjacket*, Hearthstone Pub-
> lishing, p. 64

Greed, selfishness, and financial gain are used to
compromise politicians to pass laws defeating the purpose of the Constitution, and to take America down a
path never intended by our Founding Fathers. These
politicians adopt governing principles like those of communism and the French Revolution. Following the awful bloodbath called the Civil War the nation was bleeding, and things were in disarray. The country was quite
vulnerable to more Jesuit mischief, and they took good
advantage of it.

Chapter 4

Thaddeus Stevens and the
Trashing of the Constitution

Anyone who saw the Congress of the 1860s would declare that Thaddeus Stevens was undeniably in charge.

His tremendous power as a party leader lay in the biting bitterness of his tongue and the dominating arrogance of his manner, before which weaker men shriveled. When a colleague dared question the wisdom of his policy, he replied with studied contempt that he did not 'propose either to take his counsel, recognize his authority, or believe a word he says.' His flings were consuming flame, his invective terrible to withstand... One who observed him well thought that 'the intensity of his hatred was almost next to infernal.' There were no neutral tones in his vocabulary... He had no sympathy with failure. Thus there was a hardness about him that made men dread him. Time and again he was to enter a party caucus with sentiment against him to tongue-lash his followers into line. It was easier to follow than to cross him. He had all the domineering arrogance of the traditional boss. He brooked no opposition. Schurz [A colleague of Stevens] noted even in his conversation, 'a certain absolutism of opinion with contemptuous scorn for adverse argument.' He was a dictator who handed down his decrees, and woe to the rebel who would reject him... And he could not compromise — that was at once his strength and weakness. It made him a leader while he lived, and a failure in the perspective of the years. He held no council, heeded no advice, hearkened to no warning, and with an iron will he pushed forward as his instinct bade, defying, if need be, the opinion of his time, and turning it by sheer force to his purpose. A striking figure on the canvas of history — stern, arrogant, intense, with a threatening light in his eye, and something between a sneer and a Voltairian smile upon his thin, hard lips. Such was the greatest party and congressional leader of his time. — Claude Bowers, *The Tragic Era*, AMS Press, pp. 74, 84.

He was in his sixties at the time, slowing due to age and illness, but his mind had lost none of its invective. He was not a particularly brilliant man. He made sure that everyone knew exactly where he stood, and he expected everyone to stand with him. If they did not, he made sure that they knew he was very unhappy about it. This radical, Thaddeus Stevens, controlled the Congress and applied all his overbearing and caustic manner to bring about one of the greatest revolutions in America since 1776. By his influence, certain hidden changes were implemented to the reconstruction amendments that did so much more than provide freedom and equality for the slaves, but rather attacked the very rational for the Bill of Rights.

Two years after the Constitution of the United States was ratified, the French Revolution began and shortly thereafter degenerated into mob rule. The Jesuits then proceeded to manipulate it in order to restore France back to the Catholic dictatorship. Thus, the world was treated to a very graphic illustration of a pure democracy in the French Revolution.

These two drastically different forms of government, the United States' republic and the French democracy, were revealed for all the world to see. The Constitution guaranteed Republican government where the government was founded on law, and every citizen was equal before the law. In France, however, the great cry was for democracy and mob rule.

> At that time (1789) France was the richest and most populous nation on the continent of Europe; and it was here that the 'Great Experiment in Democracy' began. The battle cry was 'liberty, equality, and fraternity.' The vehicle was Socialism. — Dee Zahner, *The Secret Side of History*, LTAA Communications Publishers, p. 34.

Let us review the definitions of a republic and democracy that we read in chapter one. A pure democracy is based solely on the majority without any restrictions on what the majority can do. An excellent example of a democracy is a lynch mob. The majority wants to hang the person, and the minority, the person to be hanged, does not want to be hanged, so they have a vote, and then hang the person. In a pure democracy, the minority is the victim of the majority.

In contrast, a Republic is founded on a set of laws that describe what the government can and cannot do. In a Republic, the law on which the government is founded protects the minority from the majority. The law on which the United States' Republic is founded is the Constitution. For instance, the Constitution says,

> Congress shall make no law respecting an establishment of religion, or prohibiting the free exercise thereof. — First amendment to the Constitution.

If a law were proposed in Congress to set up a national religion, and everyone in Congress voted for it, it still cannot be done, because the Constitution prohibits this type of law. The Constitution says that the government is not permitted to pass any law concerning religion. During the Dark Ages, over 150 million Christians were put to death because they would not abide by Catholicism, the universal religion at that time. The same thing would happen in America if America were a pure democracy.

The word democracy cannot be found in the Constitution or in the Declaration of Independence, or in any of the state's constitutions. Many of the Founders of the United States tried to warn about the dangers of a pure democracy.

> Democracies have ever been spectacles of turbulence and contention; have ever been found incompatible with personal security or the rights of property; and have in general been as short in their lives as they have been violent in their death. — James Madison, *Federalist Paper #10*.

Notice how short the French Revolution democracy was. People generally do not have a good understanding about democracy because of the lies about it told by the news media, schools, colleges, books, and even governments themselves. Nevertheless, what James Madison said about democracy is entirely true. It is nothing but mob rule.

> Remember, democracy never lasts long. It soon wastes, exhausts, and murders itself. There never was a democracy yet that did not commit suicide. — John Adams, *The Works of John Adams*, Vol. 6, New Library Press, p. 484.

If America had been established as a pure democracy, it would have long since ceased to exist.

> What we learn to-day from the study of the Great Revolution [French Revolution]…is that it was the source and origin of all the present

communist, anarchist, and socialist conceptions.
...up till now, modern socialism has added absolutely nothing to the ideas that were circulating
among the French people between 1789 and
1794... Modern socialism has only systematized
those ideas and found arguments in their favor. —
Nesta Webster, *The French Revolution*, Noontide
Press, p. 5.

The French Revolution was a source for
communist, anarchist, and socialist conceptions;
conceptions that, when carried to conclusion,
resulted in the necessity of installing drainage
systems to carry away the torrents of blood that
flowed from French guillotines. These same 'conceptions' applied during the twentieth century
have resulted in the murder of well over one
hundred million human beings. There is much to
learn from the Great Revolution. — Dee Zahner,
The Secret Side of History, LTAA Communications, page 35.

At the same time anarchy is seeking to sweep
away all law, not only divine, but human. The
centralizing of wealth and power; the vast combinations for the enriching of the few at the expense
of the many; the combinations of the poorer classes
for the defense of their interests and claims; the
spirit of unrest, of riot and bloodshed; the worldwide dissemination of the same teachings that led
to the French Revolution — all are tending to
involve the whole world in a struggle similar to that
which convulsed France. — E. G. White, *Education*, Pacific Press Publishing Association, p. 228.

Socialism, ideally, is a government where a com-
munity of people own everything equally. In actual practice, however, it is a form of government where the
government owns everything. This, of course, is the

definition of communism. Anarchy is the absence of government.

The principles of democracy or mob rule have filled this world with blood. Thaddeus Stevens was most instrumental in bringing the ideals of the French Revolution to America.

As we have seen, the ideas of Karl Marx were nothing new. He simply took the ideas of the Jesuits and Weishaupt and codified them into the Communist Manifesto.

> In actual fact the Communist Manifesto was in circulation for many years before Marx's name was widely enough recognized to establish his authorship for this revolutionary handbook. All Karl Marx really did was update and codify the very same revolutionary plans and principles set down seventy years earlier by Adam Weishaupt, the founder of the Order of the Illuminati in Bavaria. And, It is widely acknowledged by serious scholars of this subject that the League of the Just Men was simply an extension of the Illuminati. — Gary Allen, *None Dare Call it Conspiracy*, Concord Press, p. 25.

The principles of democracy, communism, and the French Revolution, codified by Karl Marx, are seen in countless countries in the twentieth century. From the purges in Russia by Josef Stalin, to Mao Tse Tung's Reign of Terror in China, to Pol Pot in Cambodia and numerous others, the results of Jesuitism have filled this world with misery, pain, suffering, and death. Will the United States, the greatest bastion of Republican government and freedom, fall as well?

After the Civil War, America was in shambles. The South had to start all over again. Over three million slaves, who had only known the cotton fields and hard labor, were now free. Carpetbaggers were pillaging an already depleted South. Abraham Lincoln, the man who guided America through the bloody Civil War, was dead from a Jesuit assassin's bullet. Great struggles faced the war-torn nation.

Lincoln, like Andrew Johnson after him, wanted to allow the seceded Southern states back into the Union, but a group in Congress called the Radical Red Republicans objected. They wanted some things changed before they would allow that. They were instrumental in having the 14th amendment added to the Constitution. The Supreme Court decisions on this amendment actually took away freedoms granted by the amendment. On the surface the 14th Amendment looks very good, but after the erroneous declarations about it were made by the Supreme Court, it became clear that freedom and equality for the Afro-American free man was used to create an entirely new citizenship, which broadened the powers of the national government and attacked the Bill of Rights by allowing the government to say who is a citizen and who is not. This was the same method used in France; the peasants were struggling under horrible difficulties so the reign of terror granted them liberty and equality. Hidden beneath this was a drive to expand the power of the government and entrench the peasants in bondage still.

Notice the following statements from justices of the Supreme Court and actual cases where the 14th Amendment was interpreted. This amendment was interpreted far beyond freedom and equality for the black man.

The following statement is from the Slaughterhouse case of 1872. Notice how the supreme court interpreted the cases in light of the 14th Amendment.

We are of the opinion that the rights claimed by these plaintiffs in error [fundamental common-law rights] if they have any existence are not privileges and immunities of citizens of the United States within the meaning of the clause of the 14th

Amendment under consideration – Slaughter-house Cases, 83 US 36, 80 (1872)

According to the first Supreme Court case in which the 14th Amendment was considered, it was interpreted to mean that the Bill of Rights would not be considered as privileges and immunities of the 14th Amendment U.S. citizenship. This stance of the Supreme Court continued and was spelled out very clearly in the subsequent cases.

The right of trial by jury in civil cases, guaranteed by the 7th Amendment and the right to bear arms, guaranteed by the 2nd Amendment, have been distinctly held not to be privileges and immunities of citizens of the United States, guaranteed by the 14th Amendment. The decision rested upon the ground that this clause of the 14th Amendment did not forbid the states to abridge the personal rights enumerated in the first eight amendments, because those rights were not within the meaning of the clause 'privileges and immunities of citizens of the United States.' — Twining v. New Jersey, 211 US 97, 105,106, (1908)

Many people, who lived during that time, recognized that the Constitution was under attack by Thaddeus Stevens and his followers. That the Constitution was under direct attack after the Civil War is apparent from the books written about that era, from the newspapers, and from the speeches made by President Andrew Johnson.

Never have American public men in responsible positions, directing the destiny of the Nation, been so brutal, hypocritical and corrupt. *The Constitution was treated as a doormat on which politicians and army officers wiped their feet after wading in the muck...* So appalling is the picture

of these revolutionary years that even historians
have preferred to overlook many essential things.
Thus, Andrew Johnson, who fought the bravest
battle for constitutional liberty and for the preservation of our institutions ever waged by an Executive, until recently was left in the pillory to which
unscrupulous gamblers for power consigned him.
...and the London 'Times' was commenting that 'it
is the Constitution rather than Mr. Johnson that is
in danger." — Claude Bowers, *The Tragic Era*,
AMS Press, [emphasis supplied], preface, p. 157.

The Constitution was a doormat for politicians to
walk on with their muddy feet! The Constitution was in
grave danger of being trashed! These are appalling statements considering the glorious, protestant principles that
Constitution represents. It is very clear, that following
the Civil War, the Constitution came under furious attack from 'American' politicians who were bent on
bringing America under the sway of the Jesuits!

Here are some excerpts from speeches made by
President Andrew Johnson. While reading these, remember that Andrew Johnson was almost removed from
office because he refused to go along with the Radical
Red Republicans and their goal of destroying the Constitution.

I love the Constitution: I intend to insist upon
its guarantees. There and there alone I intend to
plant myself, with the confident hope and belief
that if the Union remains together, in less than four
years the now triumphant party will be overthrown.
— Ibid, p. 33.

The best efforts of my life have been exerted
for the maintenance of the Constitution, the en-
forcement of the laws, and the preservation of the
Union of the States. — ibid, p. 162.

Greeted cordially at Baltimore, he had said he would rather be a free citizen than be inaugurated President 'over the ruins of the Constitution,' and 'rather be a free man than be President and be a slave.' — ibid, p. 241.

"The President stands squarely against Congress and the people," wrote the indignant Julian. "Neither Jefferson nor Jackson...ever asserted with such fearless fidelity and ringing emphasis the fundamental principles of civil liberty," said the New York World. — ibid, p. 102.

It has been my fate for the last five years to fight those who have been opposed to the Union... I intend to fight all opponents of the Constitution...to fight the enemies of this glorious Union forever and forever. — ibid, p. 132.

George P. Fletcher, Constitutional scholar and professor of jurisprudence at Columbia University, says:

The Civil War called forth a new constitutional order. At the heart of this postbellum legal order lay the Reconstruction Amendments — the Thirteenth, Fourteenth, and Fifteenth Amendments, ratified in the years 1865 to 1870. *The principles of this new legal regime are so radically different from our original Constitution, drafted in 1787, that they deserve to be recognized as a second American constitution. The new constitution established, in fact a second American Republic.* The first Constitution was based on the principles of peoplehood as a voluntary association, individual freedom, and republican elitism. The guiding premises of the second constitution were, in contrast, organic nationhood, equality of all persons, and popular democracy. *These are principles radically opposed to each other.* —George P. Fletcher, *Our Secret Constitution*, Oxford University Press, p. 2.

This professor at Columbia University recognized that the Fourteenth Amendment brought about a completely different constitution than the one established in 1787. He declared that this amendment created a new constitution. As we have seen from subsequent court cases after the passing of those amendments, that is exactly what Stevens and Rome wanted to do.

> Summing it up, by 1868 the Jesuits, with their radicals Thaddeus Stevens and Charles Sumner, had forced the Fourteenth Amendment on the peoples of the States, North and South. They had created a new nation as a result of a new citizenship. By 1872 the Jesuits, with their radicals on the Supreme Court, had made the powers of both the Federal and State governments absolute, limited only by decisions of their respective King's benches — the Federal and State Supreme Courts. The transition from a Presbyterian form of government to a Roman Catholic form of government had been accomplished. And how did they do it? By declaring that the Bill of Rights were not privileges and immunities of Fourteenth Amendment citizenship, thereby overthrowing the ancient liberties. — Eric Phelps, Vatican Assassins, Halycon Unified Services, p. 327.

> We are at a loss for words in describing the dismal, diabolical and demoralizing depravity of this singular man...he was the great tool of the Jesuits in creating their socialist-communist monster of the Twentieth Century, Fourteenth Amendment America. He was called a 'traitor' by President Johnson while he 'destroyed the government of the Old Union, changed its form and spirit, and made a new Union with new theories and new powers.' Horace Greeley, one of Stevens' masters, adds, 'We have brought all laborers to a common level...by reducing the whole working population, white and black, to a condition of serfdom.' On his deathbed this old communist

'commoner' was baptized into the Roman Catholic Institution for a job well done in obedience to the Papal Caesar's tyrannical Holy Alliance and the Black Pope's evil Council of Trent. — ibid, p. 331.

In light of the heinous and destructive work of Thaddeus Stevens and the Radical Republicans, it is easy to conclude that they were the tools of Rome in destroying the great Protestant Constitution. No more wicked and diabolical men ever walked the land of the free and the home of the brave. Further insights into the life of Thaddeus Stevens add more and more evidence of Rome's vicious involvement in the ruining of the Constitution.

Early in his life, Stevens was very poor. As a result, he always held a manifest contempt for the aristocrats and the wealthy. He always held that the wealthy were made that way because they had exploited the poor. Throughout his political career, Stevens always sided with the poor. However, in the famous conflict between Andrew Jackson and Nicholas Biddle, Stevens did a very strange thing. Jackson was siding with the common man in America, fighting against the Biddle/Rothschild/Jesuit front that sought to enslave America. One would think that Stevens would automatically side with Jackson and the common people. However, this was not the case.

This enemy of aristocracy fairly frothed with rage against the Jacksonian Democracy, and fought with fervor for the moneyed aristocracy represented by Nicholas Biddle and the Bank. In his earlier years he had been as fervent in the support of the Hamiltonian aristocracy. It is these marked contradictions in his character that make him so difficult of analysis. — Claude Bowers, *The Tragic Era*, AMS Press, p. 68.

The contradictions in Stevens can be readily understood in light of his involvment in the Jesuit – Rothschild's conspiracy. Naturally, Stevens stood with the common people, but when his masters told him otherwise, he would change his principles and do as he was told. How else would one explain the flagrant contradictions in this man?

Stevens had no religious convictions. He never attended church. However, one very interesting note about his religious life surfaces in the book by Claude Bowers.

> He attended no church, which, within itself, would have colored the general impression of his character in the community in which he lived. For the Baptists he had a certain sentimental regard due to the fact that it was the church of his mother, but he was probably a free thinker...' That his mind was a howling wilderness, so far as his sense of his obligation to God was concerned,' was the opinion of Jeremiah Black; and Senator Grimes disliked him as 'a debauchee in morals.' Even so, one of his best friends was a Catholic priest in Lancaster, with whom he liked to talk and walk; and he was tenderly fond of children, and extremely sensitive to the appeals of the poor, to whom he was unvaryingly generous. — ibid, p. 78,79.

In the light of the devilish route that Stevens took toward America and the beloved Bill of Rights, his close association with this Catholic priest would lead one to conclude that this priest had great influence over Stevens mind and served as his mentor in delineating to him exactly what path he was to follow. That Stevens undermined the Protestant Constitution declares that Stevens got the ideas from somewhere and his close association with this priest could certainly be one of the paths through which the Jesuit Order got to Stevens and twisted his willing mind!

The other great influence in Stevens life from the Catholic Church came from Lydia Smith, his maid and then live-in-lover of many years.

> In the rear of his house in Lancaster, among the fruit trees, stood a little house, occupied by Lydia Smith and her husband, a very black negro barber, with their two children, likewise black. Mrs. Smith was a mulatto, and was engaged as housekeeper for the bachelor lawyer [Stevens]. After a time the husband died, and the widow moved into the master's house, and there she lived for many years. When Stevens went to Washington, she accompanied him there. Wherever he was, there she was also…. That she was devoted to Stevens was evident to all. In time, as he grew feeble, she became indispensable, acting as a buffer between him and those who would unnecessarily sap his strength…. This assumption that she was Steven's mistress was not confined, however, to undertone gossip, which is never impressive. It was current in the press, and in no instance was the publisher rebuked or threatened with a libel suit…. The housekeeper [Smith] lived with her husband until his death, and many years later was buried by his side in the Catholic cemetery in Lancaster…. Many ascribed his deep-seated hatred for the Southern whites to the influence of Lydia. His fondness for her is shown in the fact that there is in Lancaster today a portrait of this comely mulatto from the brush of Eicholtz, a prominent painter who also did a portrait of Stevens. — ibid, pp. 80,81,83.

At his deathbed, we read:

> There were Lydia Smith and the two Sisters, Loretta and Genevieve. As he was sinking rapidly, the doctor asked him how he felt. 'Very mean, Doctor.' Then Sister Loretta asked permission to

baptize him in the Catholic faith. Lydia Smith was kneeling at the foot of the bed; the two Sisters were on their knees reading the prayers for the dying. And thus Thaddeus Stevens passed to eternity. At the moment, his hand was in that of Sister Loretta, his breast heaved, he pressed her hand, and thus the end came. A year before he had said that when sick, he would rather send a hundred miles to have her with him at the end than most ministers he knew. — ibid. p. 222.

From these statements by Bowers, we can glean many things. Stevens was very attached to Smith and obviously was living in an illicit relationship with her. Smith was a devout Roman Catholic and had a tremendous influence on Stevens. On Stevens' death-bed, he was baptized by two Catholic nuns into the Catholic faith for the great service that Stevens had performed in behalf of the Catholic Church. It is clear that the influence of the Catholic priest of Lancaster and Lydia Smith were both instrumental in bringing Thaddeus Stevens to the mind-set of undermining America's Constitution. Only in the light of eternity will the heinous crimes of these people be fully realized.

Chapter 5

TIGHTENING THE NOOSE

After the Jesuits' attempts to destroy the fledgling United States, the Jesuits concentrated on another goal that had eluded them for many years. They had desperately tried to establish a central bank under Robert Morris, Alexander Hamilton, and Nicholas Biddle, but each attempt had failed. During the devastating Civil War, Augustus Belmont, a rabid Jesuit and Rothschild agent, tried to coerce Lincoln into establishing a central bank, but Lincoln understood the damage a central bank would cause to the country, and he refused.

With new gusto and a different approach, the Jesuits and the Rothschilds tried again. They realized, as Lenin had,

> that the establishment of a central bank was 90% of communizing a nation. — Fritz Springmeier, *Bloodlines of the Illuminati*, Ambassador House, p. 268.

In the mid 1750s, the Rothschilds and the Schiffs moved into the same residence, a large duplex house in Frankfurt, Germany, where their families lived together.

> He [The father Rothschild] had five daughters and five sons.... He moved from his old house, the "Haus Zur Intertfann," to a new one, "Green Shield...." when he started making more money. Green Shield was a dual residency and the other half was occupied by the Schiff family who were to

play an important role later on as agents of the
Rothschilds. — ibid, p. 244.

About 100 years after the two families lived together
in Frankfurt, Germany, Jacob Schiff was born. He was
a wizard at finances and developed the underhanded
shrewdness of the Rothschilds. In 1865, as the Civil
War was ending, young 18-year-old Jacob left Germany
and came to America.

Ten years later he became the partner of the
Illuminati firm Kuhn, Loeb & Company. Ten years
after that he became its president. [It was here that
Schiff was] directing Rothschild and Illuminati
affairs from this seat of authority. Jacob Schiff was
also on the board of directors of Central Trust
Company, Western Union, and Wells Fargo Company. — ibid, p. 268.

Between the end of the Civil War and 1914, their
main agents in the United States were Kuhn, Loeb and
Co. and the J.P. Morgan Co.

A brief history of Kuhn, Loeb and Co. appeared in
Newsweek magazine on February 1, 1936: "Abraham
Kuhn and Solomon Loeb were general merchandise
merchants in Lafayette, Indiana, in 1850. As usual in
newly settled regions, most transactions were on credit.
They soon found out that they were bankers…. In 1867,
they established Kuhn, Loeb and Co., bankers, in New
York City, and took in a young German immigrant, Jacob
Schiff, as partner. Young Schiff had important financial connections in Europe. After ten years, Jacob Schiff
was head of Kuhn, Loeb and Co., Kuhn having died
and Loeb retired. Under Schiff's guidance, the house
brought European capital into contact with American
industry."

Schiff's 'important financial connections in Europe' were the Rothschilds and their German

representatives, the M.M. Warburg Company of Hamburg and Amsterdam. Within twenty years the Rothschilds, through their Warburg-Schiff connection, had provided the capital that enabled John D. Rockefeller to greatly expand his Standard Oil empire. They also financed the activities of Edward Harriman (Railroads) and Andrew Carnegie (Steel). — Des Griffin, *Descent Into Slavery,* Emissary Publications, pp. 36,37.

Couple that with this statement.

J.P. Morgan was brought into banking by his father, Junius Morgan, in England. The Morgans were friendly competitors with the Rothschilds and became socially close to them. Morgan's London-based firm was saved from financial ruin in 1857 by the Bank of England over which the Rothschilds held great influence. Thereafter, Morgan appears to have served as a Rothschild financial agent and went to great length to appear totally American. — G. Edward Griffin, *The Creature from Jekyll Island,* American Opinion, p. 209.

Again, in the mid 1800's another German Illuminist was sent on a mission from the House of Rothschild to accomplish a goal of this New Order for the Ages. His name was Jacob Henry Schiff (1847-1920). He came to New York first for the sole purpose of getting control of the United States monetary system. He eventually became the head of the banking firm of Kuhn, Loeb and Company. He bought Kuhn & Loeb out later with Rothschild money.

Using charity as a front to hide his Illuminati One World Government activities, Jacob Schiff became one of the most important successors of Albert Pike in leading the United States toward anarchy. As stated by Lenin earlier, one of the first goals of the communists is to get control of all monetary systems of the world. And this was to be

> Jacob Schiff's first achievement. — William Sutton,
> *The New Age Movement and Illuminati 666*, Insti-
> tute of Religious Knowledge, pp. 234, 235.

Thus, we see that the Jesuit/Rothschild conspiracy sent Jacob Schiff to the United States at the end of the Civil War to gain enough control over the American financial system that it would be impossible for America to refuse a central bank. Schiff used Jesuit/Rothschild money to finance J.P. Morgan, John D. Rockefeller, Edward Harriman, and Andrew Carnegie. Through the companies owned by these four individuals, shipping, energy, oil, transportation, railroads, imports, exports, and steel, with its associate businesses, would be involved. These financial giants branched off into so many other business enterprises that it simply boggles the mind. To say the least, the financial power gained by Jacob Schiff by 1900 was absolutely staggering! We must keep in mind the statement of F. Tupper Saussy, which says:

> Aware that the Rothschilds are an important Jew-
> ish family, I looked them up in Encyclopedia
> Judaica and discovered that they bear the title
> "Guardians of the Vatican Treasury...." The ap-
> pointment of Rothschild gave the black papacy
> [Jesuits] absolute financial privacy and secrecy.
> Who would ever search a family of orthodox Jews
> for the key to the wealth of the Roman Catholic
> Church? — F. Tupper Saussy, *Rulers of Evil*,
> Osprey Bookmakers, pp. 160, 161.

Remember that references to the "black papacy" are references to the Jesuits. The head Jesuit, the Jesuit general, is referred to quite frequently as the black pope.

In their relentless drive to abolish freedom in America without firing a shot, the Jesuits used their financial agents to so dominate American business and the banking system that they were able to push a central bank on the unsuspecting American people. This time, the central bank did not fail, and America is now plagued with the Federal Reserve Bank.

While Schiff was constantly increasing in wealth, influence, and power, the Jesuit/Rothschild conspiracy sent yet another agent, Paul Warburg, to complete the goal of establishing a central bank in America.

>At the turn of the century the Rothschilds, not satisfied with the progress being made by their American operations, sent one of their top experts, Paul Moritz Warburg, over to New York to take direct charge of their assault upon the only true champion of individual liberty and prosperity — the United States.

>At a hearing of the House Committee on Banking and Currency in 1913, Warburg revealed that he was "a member of the banking firm of Kuhn, Loeb and Co. I came to this country in 1902, having been born and educated in the banking business in Hamburg, Germany, and studied banking in London and Paris, and have gone all around the world…"

>At the end of the last century people didn't "study banking in London and Paris" and go "all around the world" unless they had a special mission to perform!

>Early in 1907, Jacob Schiff, the Rothschild-owned boss of Kuhn, Loeb and Co., in a speech to the New York Chamber of Commerce, warned that 'unless we have a Central Bank with adequate control of credit resources, this country is going to undergo the most severe and far reaching money panic in its history.'

>Shortly thereafter, the United States plunged into a monetary crisis that had all the earmarks of a skillfully planned Rothschild job. The ensuing panic financially ruined tens of thousands of innocent people across the country, and made billions

for the banking elite. The purpose for the crisis was two-fold:

1. To make a financial killing for the Insiders,

And

2. To impress on the American people the "great need" for a central bank.

Paul Warburg told the Banking and Currency Committee: "In the Panic of 1907, the first suggestion I made was, 'let us have a national clearing house' [Central Bank]. The Aldrich Plan [for a Central Bank] contains many things that are simply fundamental rules of banking. — Des Griffin, *Descent Into Slavery*, Emissary Publications, p. 37.

The [Jesuit] Illuminati interests wanted to create a Central Bank in America. They wanted to build the Federal Reserve. First, they needed a bunch of banking crises that would push public opinion towards a Federal Reserve system. These were provided by the Illuminati, including J.P.Morgan's Knickerbocker Panic of 1907. Second, they needed a favorable U.S. president in office. Rothschild agent Colonel House provided this by getting Woodrow Wilson elected. — Fritz Springmeier, *Bloodlines of the Illuminati*, Ambassador House, p. 273.

The engineered banking panic of 1907 did just what the Jesuits and the Rothschilds wanted it to do. It was made to appear that the only way to avoid another depression was to have a central bank.

To convince Congress and the public that the establishment of a banking cartel was, somehow, a measure to protect the public, the Jekyll Island strategists laid down the following plan of action:

1. Do not call it a cartel nor even a central bank.

2. Make it look like a government agency.

3. Establish regional branches to create the appearance of decentralization, not dominated by Wall Street banks.

4. Begin with a conservative structure including many sound banking principles, knowing that the provisions can be quietly altered or removed in subsequent years.

5. Use the anger caused by recent panics and bank failures to create popular demand for monetary reform.

6. Employ university professors to give the plan the appearance of academic approval.

— G. Edward Griffin, *The Creature from Jekyll Island*, American Opinion, p. 438.

Under these pretenses, the American people were ready for a central bank. The name, Federal Reserve Bank, was specifically chosen to give the impression that the bank is completely owned and operated by the U.S. government. But, in fact, this bank is completely controlled by a few of the richest bankers in the world. If people understood how the Federal Reserve Bank was going to operate, and that it would be a total monopoly in money, they would not have tolerated its creation.

The dream the Jesuits had of a central bank in America took shape at Jekyll Island. The operators and controllers of this bank are from the same groups as those who were behind the central bank in the 18th and 19th century — the Jesuits and the Rothschilds!

Only one step remained to complete the project. The Jesuits needed certain men in the White House and the government to pass the Federal Reserve Act. By 1912, they had their man in the White House, Woodrow Wilson. Since Jacob Schiff was already deeply into the financial scam, the Jesuits need another man whose expertise was politics. The man they found was Edward Mandel House. It was he who controlled Wilson and his presidency in the White House.

> Col. Edward Mandel House, of the Illuminati and whose father Thomas W. House was a Rothschild agent who got rich off the Civil War, wrote in his book Philip Dru, Administrator...that "Cynical Europe said that the North would have it appear that a war had been fought for human freedom, whereas it was fought for money." It's an interesting concept to see appear in a book by a secret Illuminati member.... Another man who appears to be connected to the Rothschilds was Thomas House, who also made his fortune slipping supplies past the U.S. naval blockade of the South. His son, Col. Edward M. House, was one of the main Illuminati figures to control America during the early 20th century. — Fritz Springmeier, *Bloodlines of the Illuminati*, Ambassador House, pp. 145, 273.

> One of the most influential men behind the scenes at this time was Colonel Edward Mandell House, personal adviser to Woodrow Wilson and, later, to F.D.R. [president Franklin Delano Roosevelt] House had close contacts with both J.P. Morgan and the old banking families of Europe. He had received several years of his schooling in England and, in later years, surrounded himself with prominent members of the Fabian Society [a Jesuit front]. Furthermore, he was a

man of great personal wealth, most of it acquired
during the War Between the States. His father,
Thomas William House, had acted as the confi-
dential American agent of unknown banking interests in London. It was commonly believed he
represented the Rothschilds. — G. Edward Griffin, *The Creature from Jekyll Island*, American
Opinion, pp. 239, 240.

These two quotes show that Edward M. House was
a key agent for the Illuminati and the Rothschilds. Since
the Illuminati is a front for the Jesuits, House was a key
Jesuit agent seeking to destroy the Constitution and to
establish papal supremacy in America.

Two more insights into the life of Edward M. House
come from Dee Zahner.

In 1912, a novel was published that had been
written by Edward Mandel House. This novel,
entitled Philip Dru: Administrator, called for "Socialism as dreamed of by Karl Marx...." It should
be remembered that the influence behind Wilson
throughout his career as president was Colonel
Edward Mandel House, the Marxist (Communist)
who founded the Council on Foreign Relations,
and the man whom Wilson called his "alter ego."
— Dee Zahner, *The Secret Side of History*, LTAA
Communications, pp. 90, 112.

House hoped to see the teachings of Karl Marx
become a living reality in America. Remember that the
teachings of Marx were the codified writings of Adam
Weishaupt, the Illuminist and Jesuit agent. According
to Woodrow Wilson's own words, he was dominated
by House while he was president! How deceitful that
the man sitting in the White House portrayed himself
to the American people as a loyal American, when in
fact, he did the bidding of America's greatest enemy —
the Jesuits of Rome!

Several books reveal the control that House had over Wilson while he was the president.

> Woodrow Wilson was the sole property of Jacob Schiff and J.P.Morgan and other internationalist bankers. But the man who was really running things in the White House was the mysterious "Col." Edward Mandel House during Wilson's term in office....
>
> It was House and the internationalist bankers who promoted Wilson as the Presidential candidate.... But it was House who converted Wilson to accept the principles of the centralization of the US Monetary System. It was House that helped promote the Presidential candidacy of Franklin D. Roosevelt. — William Sutton, *The New Age Movement and The Illuminati 666*, Institute of Religious Knowledge, p. 240.

It is widely acknowledged that Colonel House was the man who selected Wilson as a presidential candidate and who secured his nomination. He became Wilson's constant companion, and the President admitted publicly that he depended on him greatly for instruction and guidance. Many of Wilson's important appointive posts in government were hand selected by House. He and Wilson even went so far as to develop a private code so they could communicate freely over the telephone. The President himself had written: "Mr. House is my second personality. He is my independent self. His thoughts and mine are one." — G. Edward Griffin, *The Creature from Jekyll Island*, American Opinion, p. 240.

> A key individual of the New York Archbishop's control of the Democratic Party through Tammany Hall, Colonel House, known as "the holy monk", was directly involved in making Woodrow Wilson and Franklin Roosevelt presidents of the Ameri-

can empire. As Wilson's advisor and "alter ego",
he pressed for the passage of Morgan's Federal
Reserve Act. — Eric John Phelps, *Vatican Assassins*, Halycon, p. 447.

In their efforts to create a Jesuit empire in America,
Jacob Schiff, J.P.Morgan, the Rockefellers, and Edward
House were their agents. So many books refer to them
as Illuminists, international bankers, or as Marxists, but
we have seen that all of these organizations were being
used as fronts for the Jesuits, and all of them do the
bidding of the Black Pope, the Jesuit general!

The early 1900s were very busy years indeed. The
Federal Reserve Act and a central bank, World War One,
and the sinking of the Titanic were just a few of the
events transpiring at that time. Two other unfortunate
events were the toppling of Czarist Russia and the to
establishment of the League of Nations.

When the Czar of Russia, Alexander I, rejected the
Jesuits' effort to create a League of Nations in Europe,
the Jesuits wanted to destroy him and the system of
government that he represented. Coupled with this, the
Czar had always been the protector of the Russian Orthodox Church, which was the Vatican's implacable
enemy ever since 1054. Thus, the Jesuits felt that if the
Czar could be eliminated and a new government established, they would accomplish two important goals: the
Czar would be eliminated, and the Orthodox Church in
Russia would be destroyed.

The leaders of the Revolutionary forces in Russia
were Leon Trotsky, Nicolai Lenin, and Joseph Stalin.
These three men were avowed Marxists and communists. Since Marxism and Communism can be traced
back to the Illuminati and ultimately to the Jesuits
through their agent, Adam Weishaupt, it should not sur-
prise anyone that western financiers like Jacob Schiff
and the international bankers were the ones who financed the Russian Revolution. The revolutionaries

were Jesuits of Rome, and they were financed by western bankers, who were also Jesuits of Rome.

Jacob Schiff, head of the New York based Kuhn, Loeb and Co., spent $20 million on the revolution. Federal Reserve Director, William Boyce Thompson, gave the Bolsheviks $1 million. In the summer of 1917, fifteen Wall Street financiers and attorneys, led by Thompson, went to Petrograd, the center of revolutionary activity...

After the Revolution in Russia was successful, many American businessmen who supported it went into business with the Soviets. Averill Harriman formed a joint shipping firm with the Soviets. The Rockefeller family became involved in the oil business with the Soviets. From the 1920's the Rockefeller's Chase Bank financed business in the Soviet Union. Today the Rockefeller's Chase Manhattan Bank maintains a branch office at 1 Karl Marx Square in Moscow. — Dee Zahner, *The Secret Side of History*, LTAA Communications, p. 93.

It was confirmed by the New York Journal American of February 3, 1949, that Jacob Schiff gave 20 million in gold to help the final triumph of Bolshevism in Russia. — William Sutton, *The New Age Movement and The Illuminati 666*, Institute of Religious Knowledge, p. 239.

Jacob Schiff was head of the New York investment firm, Kuhn, Loeb and Co. He was one of the principal backers of the Bolshevik revolution and personally financed Trotsky's trip from New York to Russia. He was a major contributor to Woodrow Wilson's presidential campaign and an advocate for passage of the Federal Reserve Act. — G. Edward Griffin, *The Creature from Jekyll Island*, American Opinion, p. 210.

There are numerous other references to these facts that we could quote. These people were American citizens, and most of them took an oath swearing allegiance to the Constitution. Their acts in supporting a government whose principles are diametrically opposed to the Constitution is treason. How could these people do this? How could Woodrow Wilson and FDR support Communist Russia? They were all Jesuits working to destroy the United States. They worked together and supported each other because their masters in the Vatican told them to do this. A brief chart may be of help here to see the shape of world control.

The Jesuits		
Illuminism-Weishaupt	Communism-Marx	International Bankers-Schiff
French Revolution	Codified Communistic Ideas	Financed it all

The establishment of the League of Nations after World War One was very important for the Jesuits. They had been trying to establish the League ever since the early 1800s.

The first attempt in the 20th century to unite the whole world into a One World Luciferian slave unit was tried in history by these super-rich conspirators at the close of World War I. President Woodrow Wilson on January 8th, 1918 laid out a 14 point plan to Congress for lasting peace. Within this package of world peace was neatly hidden a plan for these conspirators to get all nations of the world to give up their sovereignty. It was labeled as "The League of Nations."

These modern money changers used World War I to make tons of money and as a toll to frighten the war-torn people of the world at that time into believing if all the governments of the world would unite into a One World Government, this would stop all wars between nations, and would achieve world peace and security.

The League of Nations headquarters was in Geneva, Switzerland, and it was during World

War I that our own President Woodrow Wilson in
1918 began to draw the United States citizens,
along with the rest of the world, into accepting this
sham. Eventually, with the help of 'Col.' Edward
Mandel House, 63 nations joined the League,
although the total membership at one time never
exceeded 58. However, President Wilson was
dumbfounded when he was unable to obtain the
two-thirds vote in the US Senate required for
ratification of a treaty, and the United States never
joined The League of Nations. — William Sutton,
The New Age Movement and The Illuminati 666,
Institute of Religious Knowledge, pp. 241, 242.

The Jesuits tried again. For their next effort they
set up the Council on Foreign Relations to be their front
organization in order to establish the United Nations.
The Second World War was necessary to convince the
people of the world that they needed the United Nations in order to guarantee peace in the world. The following chapter will expose the unpublicized underhanded purposes of the Council on Foreign Relations.

Chapter 6

THE CFR: ANOTHER

JESUIT FRONT

When Woodrow Wilson, under the direction of Jesuit agent, Edward Mandel House, failed to convince the American people and the United States Senate that they should join the League of Nations, the Jesuits realized that they had to make sure this refusal never happened again. For fifty years the Jesuits had been planning World War Two. This next war was planned to make sure that America would join their next League of Nations. This time it would be called the United Nations. In order to accomplish this, the Jesuits knew that they had to have greater control of the mass media outlets, more Congressmen in their pocket, more businesses had to be dominated, and the office of the President had to be controlled. When these things were accomplished, the Jesuits knew that they would have no trouble convincing a blinded and deluded American people into eventually surrendering their sovereignty to the United Nations. In order to accomplish these things, the Jesuits created the Council on Foreign Relations. This was to be another front behind which they would hide while accomplishing their subversion in America. In England they created a similar sister organization called the Royal Institute of International Affairs.

The Council on Foreign Relations was a spin-off

from the failure of the world's leaders at the end of
World War I to embrace the League of Nations as
a true world government. It became clear to the
master planners that they had been unrealistic in
their expectations for rapid acceptance. — G.
Edward Griffin, *The Creature from Jekyll Island*,
American Opinion, p. 273.

The agents of the Jesuits created the Council
on Foreign Relations. The locations would be in
the two most powerful Roman Catholic Dioceses
in the American empire, New York and Chicago.
The CFR would control the empire's finance,
government, industry, religion, education, and
press. No one could be elected to the Presidency
of the United States without the Council's con-
sent, as the office would be a tool for the Arch-
bishop of New York subject to 'the Vicar of Christ'
[the pope] in Rome. (One of the founders of the
CFR also aided in the creation of the Federal
Reserve Bank. He was the 'holy monk', a Shriner
Freemason and agent of the Jesuit General.) Its
purpose was to return the world to the Pope's Dark
Ages with an economically socialist world police
state. — Eric Phelps, *Vatican Assassins*, Halcyon
Unified Services, p. 464, 465.

And it was Edward M. House, under the watchful
eye of Jacob Schiff, who was under the watchful
eye of the HEAD of this international conspiracy
[the House of Rothschild of London and Paris],
that established in 1921 what their earlier com-
rades established, to overthrow the governments
of France and Russia. Called the Jacobin Clubs in
France in the 18th century, this aristocratic revolutionary movement today in America is called THE
COUNCIL ON FOREIGN RELATIONS, INC. and
its offshoot is the TRILATERAL COMMISSION.
The Council on Foreign Relations, Inc. is the
political side of the Illuminati today. They have
produced Congressmen, Senators and even Presi-

dents, that they have used to pass laws that have little by little led America into becoming a Socialist country... Now when the Conspirators saw that their One World Government couldn't be achieved using the name The League of Nations, Col. House, under the direction of Jacob Schiff, formed an aristocratic secret organization called the Council on Foreign Relations, Inc. This private Secret Society is to produce enough Congressmen, Senators, and Statesmen, etc. so the next attempt to incorporate the US into a One-World Government will not fail, because of the voting power they hope to have. But reader, remember, this is not a United States Government run establishment. — William Sutton, *The New Age Movement and The Illuminati 666*, The Institute of Religious Knowledge, pp. 240-242.

Phelps showed that the Jesuits created the Council on Foreign Relations. Therefore, the Council on Foreign Relations is yet another front organization of the Jesuit Order. The following chart shows the various Jesuit front organizations and the people in control of them.

The Jesuits

The Illuminati	House of Rothschild	Communism	Council on Foreign Relations
Adam Weishaupt	Jacob Schiff	Lenin	Edward Mandel House
	J.P. Morgan	Stalin	J.P. Morgan
	Rockefellers	Mao Tse Tung	Rockefellers

The Council on Foreign Relations is extremely powerful and has been very effective in carrying out the subversive goals of the Jesuits. This organization is so secretive that most people are not aware of its existence. The Council on Foreign Relations was instrumental in coercing America into the United Nations after World War II. Following the war, there was a concentrated barrage of propaganda from the news media to convince the people of America that the only way to have peace was to join the United Nations. Today, America is a member of this international governing body. Incidentally, instead of having the United Nations in Europe as they did with the League of Nations, they even managed to house the United Nations in New York City so that it would be a greater malicious influence in this country. Also, the United Nations charter is very similar to communist Russia's constitution. The charter guarantees absolutely no freedoms, although the wording sounds as if it does.

Instead of its headquarters being located in Geneva, Switzerland, this time the conspirators place it in New York City. Who donated the money to buy the land and the building materials to unite the nations? It was John D. Rockefeller who sank 18.5 million as a gift to the UN, to buy 18 acres of land along the East River in New York, where it is located today. — *The World Book Encyclopedia*, Volume 20, page 40.

At least FORTY-SEVEN C.F.R. [Council on Foreign Relations, Inc.] members were among the American delegates to the founding of the United Nations in San Francisco in 1945. Members of the CFR group included Harold Stassen, John J. McCloy, Owen Lattimore [called by the Senate Internal Security Subcommittee a 'conscious articulate instrument of the Soviet conspiracy'], Alger Hiss [Communist spy], Philip Jessup, Harry Dexter White [convicted Communist agent], Nelson Rockefeller, John Foster Dulles, John Carter Vincent [security risk], and Dean Acheson. — Gary Allen, *None Dare Call It Conspiracy*, Concord Press, p. 86.

For many years, David Rockefeller was the Chairman of the Board of this organization, the CFR. All of these men, claiming to be loyal to the American people and its constitution, made sure that America joined this organization, whose one great intention was to destroy the sovereignty of America and all other nations. These men all held positions of influence and power in the American government; all of them were considered to be seeking America's best, when in reality, they were all members of the CFR, an organization created by Jesuit agents with the sole intent of destroying America. This was their first great goal and it succeeded only too well. Consider some of their methods for subverting America.

In order to bring America into this conspiratorial body, the CFR had to maintain the utmost secrecy. The public was not aware of the existence of the CFR.

> To guard against exposure, and to mold public opinion, as far back as 1915 the powerful men in America working in world government set out to control the news media. They accomplished this by employing 12 leading men in the newspaper field to find out what was necessary to control the general policy of the daily press throughout the country. It was decided that this could be accomplished by purchasing control of 25 of the greatest papers. Thus, while the Council on Foreign Relations was working to remake the world, for the first 35 years of its existence, no feature article about it appeared in the news media. It was not until the 1960s that this near total control of the media began to be circumvented.
>
> For decades many top officials of the United States Government have been members of the Council on Foreign Relations. This includes many presidents, fourteen secretaries of state, fourteen treasury secretaries, eleven defense secretaries, and scores of other federal department heads. — Dee Zahner, *The Secret Side of History*, LTAA Communications Publishers, p. 91.

Most Americans have never heard of the Council on Foreign Relations. Although unseen and unknown, it has exerted tremendous power and control over the decision making process in America in the 21st century and throughout most of the 20th century. Some of the media organizations that show up repeatedly as being run and controlled by CFR members include NBC, CBS, ABC, New York Times, Washington Post, Des Moines Register, Los Angeles Times, Time magazine, Newsweek, Fortune, Business Week, U.S. News and World Report, the news services such as Associated Press, and many of the large, influential television stations. At least, 170 journalists are controlled by the CFR. The influence of these media giants on public opinion is phenomenal, and it is done in such a subtle way that the people are not aware that they are being conditioned what to think. The people generally believe that they are independent thinkers.

John Swinton, Chief of Staff for the New York Times, who was considered to be the dean of his profession, made a most revealing statement in 1953. At a New York Press Club dinner, Swinton declared,

> There is no such thing, at this date of the world's history, in America, as an independent press. You know it, and I know it. There is not one of you who dares to write your honest opinions, and if you did, you know beforehand that it would never appear in print. I am paid weekly for keeping my honest opinion out of the paper I am connected with. Others of you are paid similar salaries for similar things, and any of you who would be so foolish as to write honest opinions would be out on the streets looking for another job. If I allowed my honest opinions to appear in one issue of my newspaper, before twenty-four hours my occupation would be gone. *The business of the journalists is to destroy the truth; to lie outright; to pervert; to vilify; to fawn at the feet of mammon, and to sell*

his country and his race for his daily bread. You know it, and I know it and what folly is this toasting an independent press? We are the tools and vassals of rich men behind the scenes. We are the jumping jacks; they pull the strings and we dance. Our talents, our possibilities and our lives are all the property of other men. We are intellectual prostitutes. — Multiple contributors, *A U.S. Police Action: Operation Vampire Killer*, The American Citizens and Launen Association, pp. 18,19.

Swinton was honest enough to admit that he and most other journalists are told to write the things that are in harmony with the plans and purposes of the CFR. Ultimately, the world's wealthy, like the Rothschilds, Rockefellers, and Morgans, who founded and run the CFR, are under the control of the black pope, the Jesuit General in Rome. The Jesuits are using the media to prepare the world to receive the pope as the great man of peace, to receive the pope as the ruler of the world from Jerusalem, to accept the destruction of the U.S. Constitution, and to bring the world back to the feudalism of the Dark Ages.

You can see that most of what we are told about the topics and situations today are complete lies. We were emphatically told by the CFR and the Jesuit controlled politicians that the North American Free Trade Agreement, NAFTA, was in the best interests of the American people. Instead, NAFTA has destroyed thousands of middle class jobs in America and moved those jobs to Mexico and Red China. NAFTA is devastating the industrial manufacturing base in the United States. We have seen that the Jesuits are behind the effort to destroy the middle class in America and return to the structure that existed during the Dark Ages. The Jesuits want to undo everything that Protestantism and freedom has done for America, and NAFTA is part of that process.

The Jesuit run CFR has accomplished two of its goals by coercing America into the United Nations and gaining control of the mass media. Another goal of the CFR was to gain control over many U.S. corporations that would help in furthering ongoing and future projects. The following are just a few of the corporations that are controlled by the CFR and the Jesuits: Ford Motor Company, Boeing Corp., Pepsi-Cola, Heinz Co., Lockheed-Martin, Time-Warner, and Chevron. This very abbreviated list of companies makes it clear that powerful forces are being applied through the CFR to destroy America and its Constitution. Monies from these corporations and the Federal Reserve have been used to finance the Bolshevik Revolution, the rise of Adolf Hitler and the restoration of Germany, the taking over of Cuba by Fidel Castro, and the taking over of China by Mao Tse Tung, as well as the destruction of free government in Nicaragua.

> President Truman sent his Secretary of State, George Marshall, to China to pressure Chiang to form a coalition government with Mao's Communists. Marshall even wanted to send U.S. officers to train Communist guerillas. This plan was blocked by Congress. Marshall later placed an embargo on military aid to the Nationalists. Although Congress appropriated $125 million for military aid to Chiang, the Truman administration ran such interference that only a small portion of it ever reached Chiang and it proved to be too little and too late. Chiang wrote in his diary that Marshall, 'continues to try to accommodate the Communists in every possible way and force us to make concessions. He doesn't seem to care whether China survives or perishes. This indeed is a most painful situation.' Marshall was a member of the Council on Foreign Relations. — Dee Zahner, *The Secret Side of History*, LTAA Communications Publishers, p. 125.

Why did Harry Truman and George Marshall support the Communists butchers? Communist ideology is totally opposite to the American Republic established by the Constitution. Harry Truman and George Marshall were sympathetic with Mao Tse Tung because they were controlled by the same masters, the Jesuits of Rome, working through their front organization, the CFR.

The following quote shows one more example of how the Jesuits use the CFR-pro-communist fronts operating in America to destroy free governments in other countries.

> Nicaragua was a model for Latin American countries with freedom of the press, freedom of religion, private ownership of property, a free market economy, and open borders. Of all the Latin American countries, Nicaragua was among the top in human rights and living standards. Its political system was fashioned after the United States with a constitution and an electoral system based on two parties. Anyone over the age of 18 could vote.... The events that were to change Nicaragua from a free country to a slave state began one week after the inauguration of James Earl Carter as President of the United States in January 1977.... High officials in the State Department who went along with Carter's destruction of Nicaragua were: Secretary of State and CFR member Cyrus Vance, Deputy Secretary of State and CFR member Warren Christopher, Assistant Secretary of State for Human Rights and CFR member Patricia Derian, and Ambassador to Nicaragua Lawrence Pezzulo also a member of the CFR. Jimmy Carter also became a CFR member after he left the White House.
>
> Ignoring the murder of millions by the Communists, Communists that the CFR had put into power, the battle cry against Somoza [Nicaragua's very popular freely elected president] was 'human rights.' A greater example of hypocrisy would be hard to find in the annals of history.
>
> The scenario against Somoza was played out as usual, beginning with a massive smear cam-

paign by the CFR-controlled media in the United
States to condition the American people to accept
a Communist take over of Nicaragua. — Dee
Zahner, *The Secret Side of History*, LTAA Communications Publishers, pp. 131-133.

Using the CFR, the Jesuits placed their agents in
high places in the U.S. government to destroy the freedom loving Nicaraguan people and to place in power
the Communist-Jesuit, Daniel Ortega. It was from Nicaragua that Jesuit agents and CFR members, Bill Clinton
and George Bush Sr., made millions of dollars through
the drugs that were brought from Nicaragua to America.
These Jesuit-CFR agents in the U.S. government have
been working around the world destroying freedom loving republics and replacing them with Communistic
regimes that are in harmony with the goals of the Jesuits to restore temporal dominion to the pope.

The final goal of the CFR front organization of the
Jesuits was to place Jesuit agents into high places in
the American government. That this goal has been accomplished is obvious.

The CFR, which was initially dominated by J.P.
Morgan and later by the Rockefellers, is the most
powerful group in America today. It is even more
powerful than the federal government, because
almost all of the key positions in government are
held by its members. *In other words, it is the
United States government.* — G. Edward Griffin,
The Creature from Jekyll Island, American Opinion, p. 283, [emphasis supplied.]

Thus, the CFR-Jesuits run the United States today!
How can it be anything else since we are continually
bombarded by propaganda from the controlled press
and politicians? For example, they try to convince
Americans to exchange their constitutional freedoms

for security, as per the USA Patriot Act? How can it be anything else when continual attempts are made to support governments around the world that are anti-constitutional oligarchies? How can it be anything else when attempts are made to destroy the middle class in America?

Here are a few of the American officials who have sold their souls and America to ruin. These are the Benedict Arnolds of the 20th and 21st centuries. This is not a complete list by any means.

Presidents	Congressmen	Supreme Court Justices	Others
Eisenhower	Newt Gingrich	Antonin Scalia	Alan Greenspan
Jimmy Carter	Richard Gephardt	Clarence Thomas	Hubert Humphrey
George Bush Sr.	John Kerry	AnthonyKennedy	George McGovern
William Clinton	Joseph Lieberman	William Rehnquist	Henry Kissinger
George Bush Jr.	Thomas Foley		Tom Brokaw
	John Chafee		Colin Powell
			Dick Cheney

What are the ramifications of having Americans working for a foreign power in these high positions, who want to destroy this nation and everything for which it stands? They have almost accomplished the destruction of the United States.

During elections, we are given a list of candidates for which to vote. The Jesuits make sure that all these candidates are either Jesuits or sympathizers. Actually, the Jesuits control both major political parties in this country. In other words, no matter who gets into office, the CFR-Jesuits will carry out their policy through their candidates, and it makes no difference which party the candidate chooses or which candidate is elected. This means that elections are a hugh scam that is practiced on the American people in each election! From Barry Goldwater's book, we read,

When a new President comes on board, there is a great turnover in personnel, but no change in policy. Example: During the Nixon years [A Republican] Henry Kissinger, CFR member and Nelson Rockefeller's protégé, was in charge of foreign policy. When Jimmy Carter [A Democrat] was elected, Kissinger was replaced by Zbigniew Brzezinski, CFR member and David Rockefeller's protégé. — Barry Goldwater, *With No Apologies*, William Morrow & Company, p. 279.

The CFR-Jesuits have gained such control of America that their policy will be put into effect regardless of who is in office! Nearly every president since Woodrow Wilson was totally controlled by the CFR/Jesuits. The news media portrays these men as honorable, Christian, trustworthy men, but they are totally dedicated to following the treasonous CFR/Jesuit agenda. What a scam! To the unsuspecting American public, it all looks perfectly normal.

Chapter 7

VIETNAM: WHY DID WE GO?

The tragedy of America's horrible experience in Vietnam has left us with many bitter memories. Many suffer terrible bouts of depression over their experiences in Vietnam. After 40 years, many cannot hold down jobs because of the psychological trauma they experienced. The Vietnam wall in Washington, D.C. is a grim reminder that 58,000 Americans were killed in that totally unnecessary war. Why did we go?

> The word that caused so much hard feelings, disgust and hatred. Vietnam. Some call it a disgrace, some a police action. When soldiers came back battered, they were looked down upon, humiliated. The U.S. lost face in the sight of all the world. Why bring up the subject again? Because Vietnam was actually a religious war...Avro Manhattan, world authority on Vatican politics, has blown the cover on the real reason our boys suffered and died in Vietnam. He traces their death to the Vatican's passionate desire to make Asia Roman Catholic. Vatican agents hatched and plotted the Vietnam War. American soldiers were serving the Vatican in their desperate struggle to survive the jungles, the hell of warfare, pain, death and destruction. It was all engineered by the whore and her Jesuits. — Avro Manhattan, *Vietnam: why did we go?* Chick Publications, publisher's foreward.

The political and military origin of the war in

Vietnam has been described with millions of written and spoken words. Yet, nothing has been said about one of the most significant forces which contributed to its promotion, namely, the role played by religion, which in this case, means the part played by the Catholic Church, and by her diplomatic counterpart, the Vatican.

Their active participation is not mere speculation. It is an historical fact as concrete as the presence of the U.S., or the massive guerilla resistance of Asian communism. The activities of the last two have been scrutinized by thousands of books, but the former has never been assessed, not even in a summarized form.

The Catholic Church must be considered as a main promoter in the origin, escalation and prosecution of the Vietnamese conflict. From the very beginning this religious motivation helped set in motion the avalanche that was to cause endless agonies in the Asiatic and American continents... The tragedy of Vietnam will go down in history as one of the most pernicious deeds of the contemporary alliance between politics and organized religion. — ibid. p. 13.

Avro Manhattan was a world-renowned authority on the Roman Catholic Church and the almost total control they have of politics throughout the world. He was a writer for the British Broadcasting Corporation. He has laid the blame for the Vietnam war directly at the feet of the Jesuits and the papacy.

Let us look at some background information for the Vietnam War. Bo Dai, a French puppet, controlled all of Vietnam. By the early 1940s, a strong nationalism was developing throughout Vietnam. The Vietnamese wanted their country back. They wanted to get rid of the French and have total independence from all outside forces. By 1945, the freedom fighters, who were trying to drive this French puppet out of Vietnam, controlled a large part of the country. Unfortunately, the supposed freedom fighters were the Viet Minh, a very brutal communist front for Chinese and Russian communism. At the end of 1945, Bo Dai resigned, and all Vietnam managed to do was trade French control for Communist control. The Viet Minh was a group that was headed by Ho Chi Minh. Since Communism was a creation of the Jesuits, the Catholic Church felt right at home with the rule of Ho Chi Minh. However, Buddhism was the strong majority religion in Vietnam.

As Ho Chi Minh gained control of the entire area of North Vietnam, he appointed many Roman Catholics to key positions in his government. When World War II finally ended, however, France tried to step back into Vietnam again, specifically into South Vietnam. As France tried to come back into the picture after World War II, war broke out between the Ho Chi Minh controlled North Vietnamese, and the French controlled South Vietnamese.

By 1950, Harry Truman, then United States president, declared that America would finance the French in fighting the North Vietnamese. By 1954, nine countries met in Geneva, Switzerland to try to resolve the conflict. They passed an agreement stating that in two years, in 1956, general elections would be held throughout all of Vietnam, and whoever was elected would control the country. Neither the United States nor Bao Dai signed this agreement. Ho Chi Minh was very popular. If general elections were held, Ho Chi Minh would win. In fact, Dwight Eisenhower, while he was president, made a statement in which he said, "If we hold elections in Vietnam, Ho Chi Minh would get 80% of the vote." The manipulators in the American government realized that Ho Chi Minh would take over the country if elections were held. This would mean communist control of all of Vietnam

The elections were never held. The agreement to hold elections that was made in Geneva was simply ignored. Who did not want the elections to take place and why?

The military and above all the Catholic lobby-
ists in Washington set to work, determined to
persuade the United States government to prevent the election. Pope Pius XII gave full support
to their efforts. Cardinal Spellman, the Washing-
ton-Vatican go-between, was the principal spokes-
man from both. The policy of Pope Pius XII and
John Foster Dulles eventually was accepted, and
implemented, notwithstanding widespread mis-
givings in the U.S. and in Europe. — Avro Manhattan, *Vietnam: why did we go?* Chick Publications,
p. 17.

Truman, Eisenhower, and John Foster Dulles, all
members of the Jesuit controlled CFR, pushed the policy
of the papacy in spite of the fact that all Vietnam wanted
Ho Chi Minh as their independent leader. In the mid
1950s it was becoming painfully evident who was dic-
tating Vietnam policy from Washington. Most of the
congressmen who love the Constitution and the American republic were forced out of office, and Jesuits were
put in place to carry out the policies of the papacy!

To the Vatican, Vietnam was another exercise for the planting of Catholic authoritarianism in
an alien land against the wishes of the majority of
the population. The Vatican is a master at using
political and military opportunities to further its
own religious policies, which ultimately means the
expansion of the Catholic Church, which it represents. — ibid. p. 122.

While the papacy and the Jesuit controlled CFR
members in America refused to allow free elections,
they already had a simple plan ready as an alternative.

It [the Jesuit's plan] was divided into three
principal subsections: the prevention of the elections, the setting up of a man who could rule with

an iron fist, and the swift Catholicization of South Vietnam.

One of the first moves was the selection of a man fit for the task. This was ready at hand. His name was Ngo Dinh Diem. Diem had been carefully groomed by the Catholic establishment, was an ardently religious person...and a ruthless religious and political dogmatist...

Diem was a genuine believer, considered the Catholic religion the only true religion, and had dedicated his life to its maintenance and propagation. He was so religious from his earliest childhood, that at one time, he wanted to become a Catholic priest, indeed a monk. Curiously enough, he did not enter the priesthood because the life of a priest was too soft. At fifteen he spent some time in a monastery. He prayed two whole hours every day and attended mass regularly...

Diem had convinced himself that he had been chosen by God to fulfill a definite task, and that a day would come when he would be ready to carry out his mission. — ibid. pp. 55, 57.

President Ngo Dinh Diem of South Vietnam was a practicing Catholic who ruled South Vietnam with an iron fist. He was a genuine believer in the evil of communism and the uniqueness of the Catholic Church. He had originally been 'planted' into the presidency by Cardinal Spellman and Pope Pius XII. He transformed the presidency into a virtual Catholic dictatorship, ruthlessly crushing his religious and political opponents. Buddhist monks committed suicide by fire, burning themselves alive in protest against his religious persecutions. His discriminatory persecution of non-Catholics, particularly Buddhists, caused the disruption of the government and mass desertions in the army. — ibid. p. 56.

Here is how Diem created the Catholic tyranny in South Vietnam.

The next year, October 26,1956, he promulgated a new Constitution. Imitating Mussolini,
Hitler, and also Ante Pavelich of Catholic Croatia....
he inserted an article, Article 98, which gave him
full dictatorial powers. During the first legislative
term, the president (that is Diem) may decree a
temporary suspension of...(there followed almost
all the civil liberties of the nation) to meet the
legitimate demands of public security, etc. — ibid.
p. 77.

Have we heard that recently? This mistaken idea of
giving up civil liberties in order to be secure is becoming very popular. After the destruction of New York's
Twin Towers in 2001, and after the bombing at Okla-
homa City in 1995, the cry was made by Bill Clinton in
1995 and by George Bush in 2001 that in order for there
to be security in America, we need to give up some of
our liberties. Both presidents have passed unconstitutional laws and issued unconstitutional executive orders. Clinton was instrumental in passing the Omnibus
Anti terrorism Bill, and George Bush was instrumental
in passing the USA Patriot Act. Both of these acts stated
exactly what Diem said. Why? Because Diem, Clinton,
and Bush are being directed to do what they do by the
same power, the Jesuits of the Catholic Church.

The article [Article 98 from the previous quote.]
should have expired in April, 1961, but it was
maintained indefinitely. But even more danger-
ously ominous was a decree that Diem had issued
before that. In January, 1956, he had already
promulgated a personal presidential order, which
was already portending the shape of things to
come. The Order, 46, read as follows: 'Individuals
considered dangerous to the national defense
and common security may be confined by executive order to a concentration camp. — ibid. pp. 77,
79.

An obvious word was left out of that order: terrorism. That word had not yet become popular in 1956.
Today he would probably have said, "Anyone suspected
of being a terrorist and a threat to the national defense
and common security may be confined by executive
order to a concentration camp." We could, of course,
not only be talking about Diem, but also about the current President of the United States.

> Diem took the teaching of these popes liter-
> ally. For instance, he firmly held,... that it is an
> error to believe that: the church is not a true and
> perfect society. For the Church to be perfect, the
> state must be integrated with her so that the two
> become as one, because quoting again Pius IX 'it
> is an error to believe that: the church ought to be
> separated from the State and the State from the
> church' a principle, which went totally against the
> Constitution of the U.S., his sponsor. — ibid. pp.
> 82, 83.

Why was the United States agreeing with Diem,
who was going directly contrary to the principles of
our Constitution? The politicians in the United States
were directly manipulating things in Vietnam.
Eisenhower was telling Diem what he must do. The
Catholic Church through American officials such as
Eisenhower and Dulles was covertly manipulating
things in Vietnam. The Catholic Church and Cardinal
Spellman were the real problems in Vietnam.

> Elements preventing such union [union of
> church and state], therefore, had to be eliminated.
> This meant the Protestants, at that time number-
> ing about 50,000, mostly Baptists and Seventh
> Day Adventists. Diem had planned to eliminate
> them chiefly via legislation by prohibiting their
> missions, closing their schools, and refusing li-
> censes to preach, or have religious meetings.

This he would have done legally in accordance
with the future concordat to be signed with the
Vatican, modeled upon that of Franco's Spain.
Such anti-Protestant legislation would have been
enforced once the war was over and a Catholic
state had been firmly established. — ibid. p. 83.

Diem's policies brought immediate persecution.

The jails were soon bursting with prisoners.
The mass arrests became so numerous that finally it was necessary to open detention camps
followed by additional ones euphemistically called
internment camps...
There followed massacres within and outside
such detention sites, like those which took place
at Mocay, Thanhphu, Soctrang, Cangiuoc, Dailoc,
Duyxuyen, to mention only a few. Religious sects
and racial minorities were persecuted, arrested
and whenever possible eliminated. To save themselves from arrest or even death many detainees
had to accept the religion, language and customs
of the new South Vietnam, as did the minority of
Chinese and the Khmer, whose schools were
closed down. Minor groups were exterminated or
accepted the Catholic Church to save their lives.
— ibid. p. 81.

Are we reading what happened in Vietnam or the
Dark Ages? Do we recognize that the same power that
sought to annihilate all opposition to the papacy during
the Dark Ages is in virtual control in America today?
The same detention facilities, internment camps, etc.
that Diem set up in Vietnam are already in place for
when similar controls are instituted in the United States.
Blatant violations of civil liberties, of personal
freedom, multiplied by the thousands. Dissenters,
of all ages and political or religious persuasion,
were hauled off to jail or to concentration camps.
To better check the dissatisfied, every peasant

was compelled to carry an identification card. —
ibid. p. 88.

Diem was convinced that he had been raised up by
God to force the Catholic religion down the throats of
every person in South Vietnam. And if that succeeded
in South Vietnam, Diem would then take his policies
into the North and throughout all Asia. Many opposed
him, especially the Buddhists. Several pictures in
Manhattan's book show Buddhist monks at Diem's
Palace in Saigon in 1962, and prior to that, 1956 and
1957. The Buddhists realized what was going on, and
they tried to stop it by reasoning with Diem.

They first went to Diem and tried to work with him
to help him understand their plight. That didn't work,
and arrests followed. Diem's policies resulted in riots,
demonstrations, and severe persecution. Catholic
schools were attacked. Finally, some of the Buddhist
priests decided that they would make the ultimate sacrifice. They would get a large gathering together, and
in the center of this large group they would pour gasoline over their bodies and ignite themselves. That is
called self-immolation. Many pictures were taken of
Buddhist monks and priests that immolated themselves
in protest to what Diem was doing in South Vietnam.

For people to be driven to such an extent in their
protest that they would take their own lives, shows the
depths of anger and frustration these faithful Buddhist
priests were experiencing under the ruthless, Catholic
puppet, Diem!

The Catholic State machinery of suppression
became so overpowering and ruthless that even
the U.S. had to protest, privately and officially, the
bear faced religious character of Diem's Catholic
policy. The self-immolation of Buddhist monks
and nuns helped to revive the religiosity of millions
of Buddhists, who became determined to resist

the unjust laws of the Diem government. The
Catholic Church never expressed any sorrow or
admiration for these Buddhist martyrs. — ibid. p.
117.

More Buddhist demonstrations followed, all
in vain. Finally, an elderly Buddhist monk, Supe-
rior Thich Quang Duc, sent a message to President Diem. The message: "enforce a policy of
religious equality." Thereupon, having calmly sat
down in a main street of Saigon, poured gasoline
on himself and burned himself to death. It was
June 2, 1963. The self-immolation caused enormous reaction within and outside South Vietnam.
The world at large could not understand what was
going on, the media having knowingly or unknow-
ingly given muddled and contradictory reports
about the true state of affairs. — ibid. p. 113.

We see that the CFR-Jesuit controlled media was
lying to Americans about the true situation in Vietnam.
They were not telling Americans that America was funding a war in Vietnam to set up a ruthless Catholic dictator, who was trying to impose Catholicism on the country.

In spite of all the self-immolations of Buddhist
priests, Diem did not change his policy in the least. This
policy continued for several more months through October of 1963.

It is to the credit of many Americans in the civil
and military administrations, that they expressed
their horror at what they were witnessing with their
own eyes. Most of them, although confused as to
the basic issues of the religious-political conflict,
nevertheless were highly shocked at the ruthless-
ness of the Diem regime. At Washington, the
feelings were no less deep. There were recrimina-
tions and criticism. The South Vietnam religious
persecutions were threatening the domestic peace

within the U.S. itself. Besides, the rest of the world was beginning to take notice of the events by openly asking awkward questions as to the real objectives of the U.S. presence in Southeast Asia. — ibid. p. 115.

The man in the White House, John Kennedy, who had been instrumental in bringing Diem to power, and like Diem, a Roman Catholic, began to assert his authority. Kennedy saw the deplorable situation and realized that decisions had to be made. If Kennedy acted against the orders of his masters, the Jesuits, there would be definite consequences, but he went ahead and acted anyway.

Finally the U.S. issued a declaration, '...it appears that the government...of Vietnam, has instituted serious repressive measures against the Vietnamese Buddhist leaders... The U.S. deplores repressive actions of this nature.'

Notwithstanding this, and the worldwide publicity, the media of America remained strangely silent about the whole issue. When they were forced to report the news of the religious persecutions of the Buddhists by the Catholic Diem, either they gave them the smallest coverage, or minimized the whole issue when not slanting the news altogether. — ibid. p. 115.

John Kennedy was the only President in the 20th century who bucked the Jesuit Order, and he paid the ultimate price for doing what was right. He not only verbally chided South Vietnam and Diem, but he took definite action.

Subsidies to the Vietnam Special Forces were suspended. Secret directives were given to various branches closely connected with the inner links between the U.S. and the Diem regime.

Finally, on October 4th, 1963, John Richardson,
the head of the CIA in Vietnam, was abruptly
dismissed and recalled to Washington. — ibid. p.
128.

President Kennedy began a slow, but steady with-
drawal of aid from Diem. Shortly thereafter Diem and
his brother were slain on November 3, 1963.

Another Catholic leader died a short time after Diem.
On November 22, 1963, John Kennedy was shot by
multiple shooters in Dealey Plaza, Dallas, Texas. This
was one of the reasons Kennedy was shot by Jesuit
agents; he dared to do the right thing in Vietnam.

Memorandum for the President. Subject: report of McNamara-Taylor mission to South Vietnam. With this report in hand, President Kennedy
had what he wanted. It contained the essence of
decisions he had to make. He had to get reelected
to finish programs set in motion during his first
term. He had to get Americans out of Vietnam....
On November 22, 1963, the government of United
States was taken over by this superpower group
that wanted an escalation of the warfare in
Indochina and a continuing military buildup for
generations to come. — Fletcher Prouty, *JFK, the
CIA, Vietnam and the Plot to Assassinate John F.
Kennedy*, Carol Publishing Group, pp. 264, 257.

As Kennedy began to pull Americans out of Vietnam, the superpower group was greatly angered. They
plotted Kennedy's assassination, and immediately after Kennedy died, the U.S. re-escalated the awful war
in Southeast Asia. It continued for another 10 years at
enormous cost! Who was the superpower group that so
desperately wanted America to remain in Vietnam?
From the evidence we have considered, this could only
be the papacy.

> At 8:30 a.m., Saturday, the 23rd of November, 1963, the limousine carrying CIA director John McCone pulled into the White House.... He was also there to transact one piece of business prior to becoming involved in all the details entailed in a presidential transition, and the signing of National Security Memorandum 278, a classified document which immediately reversed John Kennedy's decision to withdraw from the war in Vietnam. The effect of memorandum 278 would give the Central Intelligence Agency carte blanche to proceed with a full-scale war in the Far East....
> — Robert Morrow, *First Hand Knowledge*, Shapolsky Publishers, p. 249.

This war eventually involved over half a million Americans in a life-and-death struggle without the Constitutional requirement of congressional approval. So President Kennedy began pulling troops from South Vietnam. The Catholic church strongly objected to this, and President Kennedy was gunned down. The very next day, Memorandum 278 was signed, which reversed Kennedy's decision to deescalate the war in South Vietnam.

Vietnam was a Jesuit war designed to create a Catholic superpower in Southeast Asia. The only way this could occur was by the bitter persecution of a religious giant already in the area, the Buddhists. Ngo Dinh Diem, a tyrannical Catholic dictator, was put into power. The Jesuit controlled American press said almost nothing about the terrible religious persecutions taking place in Southeast Asia. John Kennedy began pulling America out of Vietnam but was gunned down by Jesuit assassins before he could accomplish much, and the no-win war went on for another 10 years, ending in ignominious defeat for America. What remains is a winding wall in Washington, D.C., listing 58,000 Americans that lost their lives there and millions of others not listed who have lived retarded lives as a result of wounds and afflictions received in this religious war.

Jesuit wars to destroy religious enemies continue today. Next we will look at the Middle East and why do so many die near the so-called city of peace, Jerusalem?

Chapter 8

WON'T THEY EVER
STOP FIGHTING?

During the last two generations, there has been continual conflict in the Middle East. The six-day Israeli-Egyptian war of 1967, and the Yom Kippur Arab-Israeli war of 1973 are more prominent than the others. The bombings, bloodshed, crying, and the misery of war never seem to stop. Why do they continue fighting? What is the purpose of continuing this senseless killing?

The land of Israel lies at the center of an area that is completely hostile to it. Israel is of great religious and historical significance because the Messiah, Jesus Christ, walked the land of Israel for three and a half years of public ministry.

Alberto Rivera was an ex-Jesuit who revealed a tremendous amount of information about them. He has written extensively about the Jesuits and their operation in the Middle East. The Jesuits greatly maligned him because of the information he provided. This information cost him dearly. He died from poison administered by a Jesuit assassin. All Alberto's information has proven to be true.

A Jesuit cardinal named Augustine Bea showed us how desperately the Roman Catholics wanted Jerusalem at the end of the third century. Because of its religious history and its strategic location, the Holy City was considered a priceless treasure. A scheme had to be developed to make Jerusalem a Roman Catholic city.

The great untapped source of manpower that could do this job was the children of Ishmael. The poor Arabs fell victim to one of the most clever plans ever devised by the powers of darkness....

The Vatican desperately wanted Jerusalem because of its religious significance, but was blocked by the Jews. Another problem was the true Christians in North Africa preaching the gospel. Roman Catholicism was growing in power and would not tolerate any opposition. Somehow the Vatican had to create a weapon to eliminate both the Jews and the true Christian believers who refused to accept Roman Catholicism. Looking to North Africa, they saw the multitudes of Arabs as a source of manpower to do their dirty work....

The Vatican wanted to create a messiah for the Arabs, someone they could raise up as a great leader, a man with charisma who they could train, and eventually unite all the non-Catholic Arabs behind him...creating a mighty army that would ultimately capture Jerusalem for the pope. — Jack Chick, *The Prophet, Alberto part 6*, Chick Publications, pp. 5,18.

Here we see that the Catholic Church desperately wanted control of Jerusalem because of its location and its great religious significance. They wanted to use the Arabs to grind the Jews and Christians into the dust so they could take over Jerusalem. The Vatican also invented a 'messiah' figure from among the Arabs around whom the Arab world would unite.

A wealthy Arabian lady, who was a faithful follower of the pope, played a tremendous part in this drama. She was a widow named Khadijah.... Her job was to find a brilliant young man who could be used by the Vatican to create a new religion and become the messiah for the children of Ishmael. She soon found young Muhammad, and they were married.... Under orders from the Vatican, Roman Catholic Arabs across North Africa began spreading the story of a great one...who was about to rise up among the people and be the chosen one of their god. — ibid. pp. 19, 20.

Islam and the rise of Muhammad was an invention of the Catholic Church. The purpose for this new religion was the destruction of Jews and the followers of Christ in order to gain the Middle East, and especially Jerusalem for the pope.

By the time Muhammad died, the religion of Islam was exploding. The nomadic Arab tribes were joining forces in the name of Allah and his prophet, Muhammad. In their 'holy' book, the Koran, Jesus is regarded as only a prophet. If the pope was His representative on earth, then he also must be a prophet of God...which caused the followers of Muhammad to fear and respect the pope as another 'holy man.' The pope moved quickly, and issued bulls granting the Arab generals permission to invade and conquer the nations of North Africa. The Vatican helped to finance the building of these massive Islamic armies in exchange for three special favors:

1. Eliminate the Jews and Christians [which they call infidels].

2. Protect the Augustinian monks and Roman Catholics.

3. Conquer Jerusalem for 'his holiness' in the Vatican.

As time passed, the power of Islam became tremendous.... Jews and Christians were slaughtered, and Jerusalem fell into their hands.... It was

time for the pay-off.... The pope asked for Jerusalem. But by now, the Arab generals felt the exhila-
ration of victory everywhere they went. They felt
nothing could stand in their way. The pope's
carefully laid plans began to backfire, and then
crumbled before his eyes. — ibid. pp. 21, 22.

The pope's plans failed miserably. Instead of giving
Jerusalem to the pope, the Moslems built their sacred
building, Dome of the Rock, in Jerusalem on the very
site of the old Jewish temple, thus making Jerusalem
the second most holy place, next to Mecca, in the whole
Islamic world. There was no way that the victorious
and powerful Arab armies would give Jerusalem to the
pope. Now the Arab leaders turned to new lands to conquer.

The Muslim generals were determined to
conquer the world for Allah...so they turned their
eyes towards Europe. The Islamic ambassadors
approached 'His Holiness' in the Vatican and
asked for papal bulls to give them permission to
invade European countries. The Vatican was out-
raged. War was inevitable. Temporal power and
control of the world was considered the basic right
of the pope. He wouldn't think of sharing it with
what he considered heathens. The pope raised up
his armies and called them *crusades* to hold back
the children of Ishmael from grabbing Catholic
Europe. The wars continued for centuries...and
Jerusalem slipped out of the pope's grasp. — Ibid.
p. 23.

The Arab forces wanted to take over the world for
Allah. The pope said no, and wars ensued. These wars,
called crusades, went on for centuries throughout Europe and the Middle East. The papacy wanted, not only
to keep the Arabs out of Europe, but also to wrench
Jerusalem out of the hands of the Arabs. Is it possible

that the statement made by George Bush on September 17, 2001, had any historical reference? Bush declared that America was fighting a crusade against terrorism. *Is it possible that the president realized that one of the key objectives in this current war on terrorism is to regain Jerusalem for the pope? In light of Bush's track record of obedience to Rome, it should be obvious!*

U.S. *News and World Report* of April 8, 2002 has a cover title that reads, "The Crusades.... The Truth About the Epic Clash Between Christianity and Islam." The article shows that Catholicism and Islam clashed in the crusades during the Dark Ages. In this issue, when they refer to 'Christianity' they are referring to Catholicism, which is not really a Christian religion. This issue has a lengthy article that covers the crusades.

> It was the fall of 1187, and an emissary from the besieged city of Jerusalem had come to beg Saladin, the sultan of Egypt, for mercy. After barely four days of assaults, the Christian defenders saw that Saladin had them hopelessly outmatched. Waiting in his tent outside the city's walls, the Muslim ruler knew both sides had a lot riding on the outcome of this battle.
>
> For the city's defenders, the prospect of Saladin's wrath loomed. The last time Jerusalem was sacked by an invading army — a Christian one — its narrow streets ran red with blood. For Saladin, his honor depended on capturing Jerusalem. All summer his armies had battled their way north through the Christian fiefs like an angry desert wind, with only one goal: *recapturing the holy city that had been occupied by European invaders for 88 years.* — The First Holy War, U.S. *News And World Report,* April 8, 2002, p. 36, [emphasis supplied].

For nearly three centuries, the Catholic armies fought the Muslim armies for control of Jerusalem, the so-called city of peace. The Catholic armies wanted to give it to the pope as a gift because the pope wanted to rule the world from Jerusalem. The Arabs wanted it because the Dome of the Rock, their second most holy shrine, was located there.

Saladin doesn't get much play in Western history books. You're more likely to read about Richard the Lion-Hearted, the leader of the European expedition to retake Jerusalem — and even he is most often remembered as a peripheral character in Robin Hood tales....

The battle between Saladin and Richard marked the high point of the Crusades, the first major clash between Islam and Western Christendom, which lasted more than three centuries.

From their beginnings in 1095, the crusades inspired more passion than anyone expected. The first Crusade was preceded by droughts and famine and heralded by meteor showers. *The idea of an expedition to reclaim Jerusalem from the unbelievers* seized the imagination of people from all social classes. Led by deeply religious knights like Godfrey of Bouillon and Tancred, armies of 'Latin' Christians [followers of the Catholic Church] from France, Germany, England, and elsewhere marched through what is now Hungary to Constantinople, the great center of Christianity in the East. — ibid. p. 38, (emphasis supplied).

The First Crusade was really the only one that the papacy won. Blood ran knee-high through the streets of Jerusalem as the Arabs were slaughtered. This, however, would be the only victory for the papacy. Thereafter, the Muslims dominated the fighting.

Following the First Crusade,

it took almost a century before a leader strong enough to unite the Muslim Middle East appeared. When Saladin finally retook Jerusalem, it was

Christendom's turn to be shocked. The arch-bishop of Tyre, a Christian [Catholic] stronghold north of Jerusalem, hurried west to Italy on a black-sailed ship with news of Jerusalem's fall, along with letters begging for help. — ibid. p. 38.

The letters for help brought to their aid Richard the Lion-Hearted, England's most temperamental sovereign.

He arrived in the Holy Land in 1191 at the age of 33.... For 16 months, Saladin and Richard battled across the parched plains of the Holy Land. Finally, ill and leading an exhausted army, Richard negotiated a truce with Saladin and headed home. He never returned. — ibid. p. 39.

The truce permitted the crusaders to occupy a strip of land along the coast and permitted the Muslims to continue to occupy Jerusalem, but allowed Christians to visit Jerusalem.

While the crusades of the Dark Ages failed to obtain control of Jerusalem for the pope, the most recent wars in the last 100 years have brought the papacy closer to her goal than she ever has been.

Marching into a Jerusalem captured from the Turks in 1917, a British general, Sir Edmund Allenby, proudly declared 'today the wars of the Crusaders are completed,' and the British press celebrated his victory with cartoons of Richard the Lion-Hearted looking down at Jerusalem above the caption 'At last my dream come true.' The colonial powers glorified the Crusaders as their ideological forebears. — ibid, p. 39.

During WW I, the papacy, still with a strong desire for control of Jerusalem, planned a sequence of events that would finally allow the papacy to take over Jerusalem. Using nations under her control, among whom was Britain, the papacy took control of the Holy Land from the Muslim Turks. This was step 1 in the process.

England was to take Palestine away from the Turks. This resulted in the creation of a national homeland for the Jews with the Balfour Declaration. During World War II, the Jesuits would not allow the trapped European Jews to emigrate to Roosevelt's American Empire, Churchill's Great Britain or Stalin's Russian Empire. Rather, the Order permitted many to enter Palestine while the majority perished in the Death Camps located deep in the woods of Roman Catholic, Jesuit-controlled, Poland... By 1918, the order, financed by its Federal Reserve Bank and Bank of England, will have completed the first phase of its Second Thirty Years' War — World War I, including the Great Influenza Pandemic of 1918 having globally killed forty to one hundred million people. *During that time the Jesuit General will have used his British Intelligence Service and Lawrence of Arabia to unite the Arabs of Palestine in driving out the Ottoman Turks. He will have used General Allenby to drive the Turkish Moslems out of Jerusalem — a major accomplishment.*

And how would the Company maintain control of Palestine and Jerusalem won by its British sword? Enter the House of Rothschild with the Jewish Masonic Zionists.

In 1918, the Jesuits would cause their Zionists in England to issue the Balfour Declaration declaring Palestine to be the new homeland for 'The Wandering Jew'. Could it be that after nineteen hundred years of Rome's crusades, inquisitions and pogroms the Jewish Race would now have a place to call its own? Or was Zionism a setup for the greatest betrayal the Jewish Race has ever known.... World War I prepared the Land for the People. World War II prepared the People

for the Land. — Eric Phelps, *Vatican Assassins*,
Halycon Unified Services, pp. 464, 512, 514.

    Instead of taking a public stand, he [Spellman]
would operate behind the scenes by 'personally
calling on every South American country to cast
their votes for Israel.... There was little doubt that
Spellman knew U.N. delegates.... After a bitter
struggle, Israel was admitted to the United Nations by a vote of thirty-seven to twelve. The
Israelis had turned to a number of men of prominence, including John Foster Dulles to promote
their cause. Many were convinced that Spellman
had been the deciding factor. — John Cooney,
The American Pope, Times Books, pp. 186,187.

We have seen that the Jesuits place great significance on Israel and have fought two major wars and
numerous battles because of Israel. When we look at
history and the papacy's great desire to rule the world
from Jerusalem, future wars planned by the Jesuits and
the Illuminati will be used as further attempts to bring
the pope to Jerusalem to rule the world from there.

Their plan is that when the terrorism and killing
get bad enough, the Jesuit controlled news media will
urge upon the blinded masses the need for a peace maker
to come to that troubled area to rule. This peacemaker
will be the pope. Once he is enthroned in Jerusalem,
the 1,700-year old dream of the papacy will come true.

General Allenby declared upon entering Jerusalem
that the wars of the crusades are completed. This was
near the end of World War I. General Eisenhower, commander of the Allied forces in Europe during World
War two, declared that he was fighting a crusade in
Europe. George Bush in 2001 declared that a crusade
was being fought against terrorism. In light of Albert
Pike's statement requiring three world wars, do you
suppose that each of these men recognized the signifi-

cance of these three wars on regaining Jerusalem for the pope?

Will there ever be peace in Israel? There will probably be peace for a brief interval when the pope is enthroned there. But the pope will soon thereafter start to exercise his authority to force the entire world to become Catholic as he did during the Dark Ages when he controlled the world. This will bring about terrible persecution and destruction throughout the earth.

Chapter 9

TREASON IN HIGH PLACES

We have seen from history that the Illuminati was established by the Jesuit Order as a front organization behind which the Jesuits could operate and continue to conceal their actions from the eyes of humanity. We have also seen that the Council on Foreign Relations is another of their front organizations, created to have a high level air of respectability so that people in government could join them without having a stigma of subversion attached to them.

Another such group, but on a much smaller scale, is the exclusive Skull and Bones fraternity at Yale University. Few realize the global implications of being part of this organization. This organization is one of the paths to membership in the Illuminati.

> The Taft family (which is also related to George Bush by blood) and the Harriman family are two families that have been intimately connected to the *Skull and Bones Order (which is an entry point into the Illuminati* and on the surface just an exclusive fraternity). — Fritz Springmeier, *Bloodlines of the Illuminati*, Ambassador House, p. 320.

The Skull and Bones is one of the entry points into the Illuminati. The Illuminati, which we have seen, is a front for the Jesuits. Anyone who is working for the Illuminati or their purposes is associated with the Jesuits, the greatest foe of Protestant religious and civil liberty. To be part of the Illuminati and the Jesuits makes it impossible to love the U.S. Constitution or to uphold its principles because those groups exist for the purpose of destroying the Constitution. No president or public official in America could ever be part of these groups because it would be impossible to uphold their oath of office to defend the U.S. Constitution. Those in office who have betrayed this oath are traitors because they are part of organizations whose goal is the abolishment of that great document.

Are you aware of any leaders or Presidents that have ever held office who have been part of the Skull and Bones Order of Yale University?

> "George Bush (father and son) was a Skull and Bonesman.... George Bush also is a descendent of the 13th top Illuminati family — the family that ties in with British royalty and the Merovingians."
> — ibid. page 320.

George Bush, the father, and George Bush, the son, have both attended Yale University, and both joined the Skull and Bones Order. Both of these men are part of the Illuminati and the Jesuits. Both of these men, because of their membership in these organizations, should have been disqualified from being Presidents of the United States. We have seen that members of these groups are working for the destruction of America and its Constitution rather than working to defend the Protestant principles and freedoms upon which this country was founded. No member of these organizations should ever be permitted to occupy any position in the American government, but those in the government who are members of these groups are being told by their handlers to slowly but surely destroy this great land! America is in very serious trouble as is becoming quite obvious today.

The Bush family's connection to the Harriman's/Illuminati/Jesuits goes way back.

Cornelius Vanderbilt Whitney married Marie Norton who later married W. Averell Harriman (initiated Into Skull & Bones in 1913), the man who helped finance Hitler to power. The Harrimans also helped bring the Bush family from oblivion back in the early 1920's. When Prescott Bush (George Bush's father) lost all his money in the 1929 stock market crash, the Harrimans again came to financially help Prescott Bush back on his feet. During the 1920's, the W. Averell Harriman, Prescott Bush , Fritz Thyssen and Friedrich Flick created several entities to help finance Hitler and to produce the weapons Hitler would need to fight W. W. II. — ibid. page 63.

The Bush family has been connected with the Illuminati/Jesuits for the last 85 years. The resulting influence they have had on the policies of both George Bush, father and son, have only aided the Illuminati/Jesuits in their ongoing efforts to destroy the Constitution and America.

Before George Bush ever entered the White House in January of 2001, he was already vowing his support for the work of the Catholic Church in America. He showed that his allegiance would not be to the Constitution and the American people, but rather to a man (the popes) whose position over the last 200 plus years has been the destruction of the Constitution and America.

In 1960, John Kennedy went from Washington to Texas to assure Protestant preachers that he would not obey the pope. In 2001, George Bush came from Texas up to Washington to assure a group of Catholic Bishops that he would obey the pope. — *Washington Times*, April 16,2001.

The President of the United States is not running the United States. A foreign dictator, who was respon-

sible for slaughtering millions of people, and who is
working for the destruction of this country, is telling
the President what to do, and he is happy to do it! That
is truly a shocking and revolting revelation.

> The pope is the ruler of the world. All the emper-
> ors, all the kings, all the princes, all the presidents
> of the world are as these altar boys of mine. —
> Priest Phelan, Western Watchman, June 27, 1912.

Notice that that last quote is from a Catholic publication. Emperors, kings, princes, and Presidents are as
altar boys for the pope. What does an altar boy do? An
altar boy is a willing and obedient servant/slave to the
priest. When the priest tells the altar boy to do something, the altar boy does not ask any questions, but car-
ries out exactly what the priest told him to do. For hundreds of years, the leaders of the world have been doing the pope's bidding. According to the article in the
Washington Times, which we just read, the president
of the United States is a willing servant to the pope.

Shortly after becoming president in 2001, George
Bush dedicated a cultural center in Washington, DC to
pope John Paul II. This is what the president said at the
dedication of this memorial.

> The best way to honor Pope John Paul II, truly one
> of the great men, is to take his teachings seriously,
> to listen to his words and put his words and
> teachings into action here in America. — Reuters
> News Service, March 22, 2001.

The president of the United States said that we need
to put the words and teachings of the pope into action
here in America. If the president, indeed, did this, as he
said he would, it would result in the complete destruction of this country and its constitution. From the very
inception of the United States, the Catholic church and

the Jesuits have wanted to destroy this nation, and have wanted to abolish its Constitution. George Bush took a solemn oath that he would protect and defend the Constitution. By his declaration at the dedication of the cultural center, he has vowed to ignore his oath of office and carry out the dictates of the pope, who is working for the destruction of America.

> Treason doth never prosper: what's the reason? For if it prosper, none dare call it treason. — John A. Stormer

Let us now compare the statements of the pope and the Jesuits with what the U. S. Constitution says.

> The most sacred principle of the United States Constitution is the equality of every citizen before the law. The fundamental principle of the church of Rome is the denial of that equality. Liberty of conscience is proclaimed by the United States, a most sacred principle which every citizen must uphold... But liberty of conscience is declared by all the popes and councils of Rome, a most of godless, unholy, and diabolical thing, which every good Catholic must abhor and destroy at any cost. — Charles Chiniquy, *Fifty Years in the Church of Rome* , page 284.

So by George Bush's statements at the dedication of the cultural Center, he would abolish the freedoms guaranteed to the people of the United States by the Constitution.

> The American Constitution assures the absolute independence of the civil from the ecclesiastical or church power; but the Church of Rome declares through all her pontiffs and councils that such independence is an impiety and revolt against God. — Ibid, p. 284.

The first amendment of the Constitution demands the separation of the churches from the state, but the Catholic church throughout the dark ages and today has been trying to combine them. The result of such a union has always been terrible bloodshed and persecution. The founding fathers realized the dangers of uniting the church with the state, and they made sure in the Bill of Rights that the church and state would remain separate.

> Congress shall make no law respecting an establishment of religion, or prohibiting the free exercise thereof; or abridging the freedom of speech, or of the press, or the right of the people peaceably to assemble, and to petition the Government for a redress of grievances. — First Amendment, The Constitution of the United States.

> The American Constitution leaves every man free to serve God according to the dictates of his own conscience; but the Church of Rome declares that no man has ever had such a right, and that the pope alone can know and say what man must believe and do. Ibid, p. 284.

That is absolute insanity that another man believes that he has the right to tell someone what they can believe and what they can do. That is utter blasphemy.

> The Constitution of the United States denies the right in anybody to punish any other for differing from him in religion. But the church of Rome says that she has the right to punish with the confiscation of their goods, or the penalty of death, those who differ in faith from the pope. — Ibid, p. 284.

What a tragedy. During the Dark Ages, the papacy slaughtered over 200 million people because they wanted to worship God according to the Bible. How many beliefs of the pope and the Catholic church are even found in the word of God? Is purgatory in the Bible? Is the worship of the Virgin Mary in the Bible? Is turning the bread in the communion service into the actual body of Christ in the Bible? Of course it is not. The papacy declares that the pope can punish and even kill those who believe the Bible.

History has shown how one pope after another differed from previous popes. There have been rival popes, two or three at one time, disagreeing with each other. Which infallible pope are we to accept? For a human being to bow down and receive their faith from a man who does not know what he believes is utter insanity!

> The Constitution of the United States is based on the principle that the people are the primary source of all civil power. [It's a government of the people by the people and for the people]. But hundreds of times, the Church of Rome has proclaimed that this principle is impious and heretical. She says that "all government must rest upon the foundation of the Catholic faith; with the pope alone as the legitimate and infallible source and interpreter of the law." — ibid, p. 284

We are entering a time in earth's history, when the blood of conscientious Christians will flow across this land as it did throughout Europe during the Dark Ages. George Bush's words at the dedication of the cultural center will take us to the Dark Ages again.

After the destruction of the twin towers in New York on September 11, George Bush did not act as a loyal American president defending the Constitution. We wish he had. Instead, George Bush's response to the terrorist attack of September 11 was the passage of his USA Patriot Act, which essentially threw out the Bill of Rights and other parts of the Constitution that guaranteed freedoms.

How could the Congress have voted on such a law? During the deliberations a bill was arrived at that both the House and Senate agreed upon. Even the liberals and conservatives agreed on this bill. But, on the morning before the scheduled vote, a different bill — with the same name, of course, and which was printed at three o'clock in the morning before the vote — was substituted for the bill the congress approved. Not one member of the House or Senate read the substituted bill. Many probably did not even know that a different bill was substituted. The bill that was passed was this substituted bill, which President Bush readily signed into law. — This information is from the documentary movie entitled *Unconstitutional: The War On Our Civil Liberties*. This movie contains members of Congress speaking to expose this blatant disregard of our Constitution.

> President Bush signed new [so-called] anti-terror laws on Friday, aggressively expanding the US government's power to hold immigrants without charges, eavesdrop on electronic communications, and crack money-laundering schemes.
> Bush said, "Today, we take an essential step in defeating terrorism while protecting the constitutional rights of all Americans."
> Crafted in response to the Sept. 11 attacks on the United States, the bill enhances the ability of federal authorities to tap phones, share intelligence information, track Internet usage, e-mails and cell phones and protect U.S. borders. — Patricia Wilson, Reuters News Service, October 26, 2001.

The president passes an act that guts the Constitutional rights of Americans. He gives federal agencies the authority to read your e-mail before you do, to listen to your phone conversations, and then he has the audacity to tell Americans, "We are destroying all your liberties, but don't worry, we won't bother your constitutional rights." Does he think we are idiots?

In the same article, we read a quote from Laura Murphy, the director of the American Civil Liberties Union.

> We can not as a nation allow very legitimate public anxiety to immunize the administration and Congress from their obligation to protect the Bill of Rights and the fundamental values that document embodies. — ibid, 2001.

She understood that the USA Patriot Act would annihilate our basic freedoms.

In the name of fighting terrorism the president is taking away our civil liberties that Americans have enjoyed since the birth of our nation. With all our freedoms gone, will that somehow make terrorism go away? Instead of making terrorism go away, it will simply transfer the source of terrorism from the middle east to the United States Government. Terrorism has never been adequately defined. The United States will become a ruthless persecuting government, and whoever the government says is a terrorist will be persecuted.

In yet another Associated Press article, we read:

> Attorney General John Ashcroft ordered Federal prosecutors Friday to use new anti-terrorism powers to track down terrorists by intercepting their Internet and telephone communications and financial transactions....
>
> Under the new law, prosecutors have more powers to eavesdrop on suspected terrorists, wherever they are and whether they are communicating on the Internet or by phone.
>
> On Thursday, Ashcroft warned would-be terrorists that the government will be closely watching how they act, carefully listening to what they say and secretly reading the words they write.
>
> He pledged to use the new powers granted by

Congress to pursue terrorist suspects relentlessly,
intercept their phone calls, read their unopened e-
mail and phone messages, and throw them in jail
for the smallest crimes. — Karen Gullo, *Feds Vow
to Use Anti-Terror Tools*, October 26, 2001.

We must again emphasize strongly that the word
"terrorism" has not been adequately defined. When
someone does something that is perfectly legal under
the Constitution, but the government doesn't like it, that
person could be labeled a terrorist and severely persecuted under the Patriot Act.

The Patriot Act was passed because of Illuminati/
Jesuit instructions to Washington's government officials
and was a direct assault on the Bill of Rights, the first
10 amendments to our Constitution.

In whose name are all these things being done? On
the cover of Newsweek, March 10, 2003, the president
is praying. The cover says that, "Faith Changed His Life
and Shaped His Presidency;" The American people are
being told that God is guiding the President, but he is
acting in ways that will destroy our God-given Constitution and bring America under the iron fist of the papacy. As far as Bush's domestic programs are concerned
they all reflect the teachings of the papacy. The
Newsweek magazine relates that the President was aided
in these programs by John Dilulio, who tutored him in
the philosophy of Catholic social doctrine. (Newsweek,
March 10, 2003, page 29)

Our God-given Constitution does not need changes
the way the president is attempting. What is needed is
for the president to start abiding by his oath of office
and uphold and support the Constitution by throwing
out the Patriotic Act and other subversive and illegal
legislation. God is in no way helping the president to
destroy our Constitution.

While it is clear that the President is being led by a god, it certainly is not the God in heaven, but rather the god on his throne in Rome! Before ever reaching the White House, the president promised Catholic bishops that he would obey the pope, and he is certainly keeping his word. The president of the United States is obeying Protestant America's greatest enemy. This nation and the Constitution and are in very grave danger.

Chapter 10

THE WAR ON TERROR WAS PLANNED 135 YEARS AGO

The basis for this entire chapter is a letter that was written August 15, 1871 by Albert Pike to Giusseppe Mazzini, as quoted in the book, *Descent into Slavery*.

Having consolidated their financial grip on most of the European nations by the middle of the last century, the International Bankers worked feverishly to extend their sphere of influence to the ends of the earth in preparation for their final assault on the United States — a nation which, through its unique Constitution, remained free.

In the decades that followed it became apparent that, in order to achieve their goal of world domination, they would have to instigate a series of wars which would result in the leveling of the old world order in preparation for the construction of the New World Order. This plan was outlined in graphic detail by Albert Pike, the Sovereign Grand Commander of the Ancient and Accepted Scottish Rite of Freemasonry and the top Illuminist in America, in a letter to Giusseppe Mazzini dated August 15, 1871. Pike stated that the first world war was to be fomented in order to destroy Czarist Russia and to place that vast land under the direct control of Illuminati agents. Russia was then to be used as a 'bogey man' to further the aims of the Illuminati worldwide.

World War II was to be fomented through manipulation of the differences that existed between the German Nationalists and the Political Zionists. This was to result in an expansion of Russian influence and the establishment of a state of Israel in Palestine.

The Third World War was planned to result from the differences stirred up by Illuminati agents between the Zionists and the Arabs. The conflict was planned to spread worldwide. The Illuminati, said the letter, planned to 'unleash the Nihilists and Atheists' and 'provoke a formidable social cataclysm which in all its horror will show clearly to the nations the effect of absolute atheism, origin of savagry and of the most bloody turmoil. Then everywhere, the citizens, obliged to defend themselves against the world minority of revolutionaries, will exterminate those destroyers of civilization, and the multitude, disillusioned with Christianity, whose deistic spirits will from that moment be without compass [direction], anxious for an ideal, but without knowing where to render its adoration, will receive the true light through the universal manifestation of the pure doctrine of Lucifer, brought finally out in the public view, a manifestation which will result from the general reactionary movement which will follow the destruction of Christianity and atheism, both conquered and exterminated at the same time." — Des Griffin, *Descent Into Slavery*, Emissary Publications, pages 38,39.

We have seen that Adam Weishaupt established the Illuminati to be a front for the Jesuit Order in 1776, and that the Illuminati's operating principles are the same as the Jesuits. Weishaupt was teaching Catholic Canon Law, in a Jesuit University, in the Jesuit stronghold of Bavaria Germany, when he received the order from Jesuit General Ricci to form the Illuminati. The Jesuits then operated through the Illuminati so that the Jesuits and the Catholic Church would be kept in the background and would not be blamed for their subversive activities.

The International Bankers, which were controlled by the Jesuits as well, funded the establishment and the operation of the Illuminati. Saussy's book, *Rulers of Evil* , pages 160,161, shows that the Rothschilds and the Jesuits are partners in seeking the takeover of the world. Griffin shows that the Illuminati and the International Bankers are the ones planning these wars for world takeover, but as we have seen the Jesuits are ultimately behind and controlling this effort.

Griffin declares that Albert Pike was the top Illuminist in America. We must understand that as the top Illuminist, Pike was under the control of the Jesuits, was doing their bidding, and was knowledgeable of their most secret plans.

When Pike speaks of three world wars, he is revealing the Jesuit's plan for world control. As far back as 1871, the Jesuit Order had planned the wars of the 20th century and the current war on terror. Very few realize the extent that we have been lied to. It was not the shooting of the Archduke of Austria that caused World War I as was claimed; nor was it Adolf Hitler, Benito Mussolini, and Japan that caused World War II as was claimed; nor was it the twin towers and the weapons of mass destruction of Saddam Hussein that caused this current war on terror. These were the excuses given to the world for these wars. These wars have been conceived and thoroughly planned by the Jesuits over 130 years ago. To them and to them alone falls the responsibility for these tragedies. The visible leaders that are paraded before the world are mere puppets whose strings are being pulled by their Jesuit masters!

Pike declared that the First World War would be used to destroy Czarist Russia and then to place that land under the control of Illuminati agents. History shows that Czarist Russia was destroyed by WWI, giving control to the Illuminati. To most people, the reason why the Jesuits wanted to destroy Russia is not clear.

For well over 100 years before WWI, Czar Alexander expelled the Jesuits from Russia. Thereafter the Jesuits were greatly motivated to destroy Czarist Russia.

> The Russian emperor, Alexander, was currently compelled to issue a royal decree in 1816, by which he expelled them [the Jesuits] from St. Petersburg and Moscow. This proving ineffectual, he issued another in 1820, excluding them entirely from the Russian dominions. — R. W. Thompson, *The Footprints of the Jesuits,* Hunt and Eaton, pages 245,246.

Five years later, Alexander was poisoned to death. He wasn't the only czar to oppose the Jesuits.

> Alexander [II] had progressed well with his great reforms and had attached his signature to a Constitution to be adopted by Russia. The next day a bomb was thrown at his carriage, which killed and wounded a number of Cossacks, who accompanied the carriage. The Emperor in deep sympathy left the carriage to look at the dying men, when a second bomb blew him to pieces. — Arno Gaebelien, *Conflict of the Ages*, The Exhorters, page 85.

This same czar, who had the audacity to bring a constitution to the Russian people, also did something else for which the Jesuits would not forgive him. At the height of the Civil War, when the balance of the war could go either way, Alexander II came to the aid of Abraham Lincoln.

> It was a masterful move that possibly could have won the game had not an unexpected event tipped the scale against it. Tsar Alexander II, who, incidentally, had never allowed a central bank to

be established in Russia, notified Lincoln that he stood ready to militarily align with the North...The presence of the Russian Navy helped the Union enforce a devastating naval blockade against the Southern states which denied them access to critical supplies from Europe...The fact that neither France nor England at that time wanted to risk becoming involved in an open war with the United States and Russia led them to be extremely cautious with overt military aid to the South. Throughout the entire conflict, they found it expedient to remain officially neutral. Without the inhibiting effect of the presence of the Russian fleet, the course of the war could have been significantly different. — G. Edward Griffin, *The Creature from Jekyll Island*, American Opinion Publishing, pp 377,378.

By driving the Jesuits from Russia, refusing to establish a central bank, planning a constitution, and aiding the North during the Civil War, the czars of Russia had incurred the undying wrath of the Jesuit Order. Furthermore, the czars protected the Russian Orthodox Church, the implacable enemy of the Catholic Church for over 1000 years. Payback was imminent.

The overthrow of the Czarist system therefore, brought with it the inevitable overthrow of the established Orthodox Church. To the Vatican, which had waged war against the Orthodox Church since the eleventh century, the downfall of her millenarian rival was too good to be true. — Avro Manhattan, *The Vatican Billions*, Chick Publications, pp 120,121.

Not only was the czarist system in Russia to be destroyed, but the Orthodox Church would be toppled as well. Pike revealed that Illuminati agents would be put into positions of power in Russia. Illuminati agents, acting as a front for the evil deeds of the Jesuits, would bring an awful reign of terror to that great land for several generations. Starting with Lenin, Trotsky, and Stalin, the Jesuits used them to have millions of Russians killed for the next 30 odd years. Kruschev and Breshnev continued the onslaught to a lesser degree. All of this was done in the name of Communism, but in truth, the Jesuits used the Communist front to carry out their heinous crimes in Russia.

Ever since its beginning, America had never engaged in a war overseas. The Monroe Doctrine had declared that America would not fight foreign wars and would not look kindly on European advances in the Western Hemisphere. In order to bring America into World War I and thus violate the famed Monroe doctrine, there was a planned 'terrorist' attack that caused the loss of many American lives, and thus, bring America into the war.

The terrorist attack that was carried out against innocent Americans was called the bombing of the Lusitania.

> The Lusitania was built to military specifications and was registered with the British Admiralty as an armed auxiliary cruiser. She carried passengers as a cover to conceal her real mission, which was to bring contraband war materials from the United States. This fact was known to [Woodrow] Wilson and others in his administration, but they did nothing to stop it. When the German embassy tried to publish a warning to American passengers, the State Department intervened and prevented newspapers from printing it. When the Lusitania left New York harbor on her final voyage, she was virtually a floating ammunition depot.
>
> The British knew that to draw the United States into the war would mean the difference between defeat and victory, and anything that could accomplish that was proper, even the coldly

calculated sacrifice of one of her great ships with Englishmen abroad. *But the trick was to have Americans on board also in order to create the proper emotional climate in the United States.* As the Lusitania moved into hostile waters, where a German U-boat was known to be operating, First Lord of the Admiralty, Winston Churchill, ordered her destroyer to abandon her. This, plus the fact that she had been ordered to travel at reduced speed, made her an easy target. After the impact of one well placed torpedo, a mighty second explosion *from within* ripped her apart, and the ship that many believed could not be sunk, gurgled to the bottom in less than eighteen minutes.

The deed had been done, and it set in motion great waves of revulsion against the Germans. These waves eventually flooded through Washington and swept the United States into war. — G. Edward Griffin, The Creature From Jekyll Island, American Opinion Publishing, pp 260, 261. (Emphasis supplied.)

Does that sound familiar? Is the author talking about WWI, or WWII at Pearl Harbor, or about September 11 and the war on terror? In every case, the situation has been nearly identical. Create a fervor of anger against a foreign power, and America goes to war. And it was all planned that way! The Jesuits, who pre-planned the war, planned for the terrorist attacks in order to bring America into the battle!

The second explosion that Griffin described in the previous quote was caused by all the munitions the ship was carrying that exploded when the torpedo hit.

What about Pearl Harbor? Did 'American' leaders, who were doing the bidding of the Jesuits, have any idea that Japan would attack? Did 'American' leaders do anything to stir up the Japanese to bring on the terrorist attack at Pearl Harbor and bring America into war? In a book written by Congressman Hamilton Fish, we read,

President Roosevelt's responsibility for goading the Japanese into war by sending a war ultimatum on November 26, 1941, demanding that the Japanese withdraw all troops from Indo-China, and China (Manchuria) is an historic fact, although a closely-guarded secret.

FDR's war ultimatum was deliberately withheld from Congress until after Pearl Harbor...all agreed that the ultimatum left Japan no alternative but war...

The Japanese would have done almost anything to avoid war with America...

Prince Kenoye, the prime minister, who was very peacefully inclined, repeatedly requested to come to Washington or Honolulu to meet with President Roosevelt. He was willing to agree to our terms to keep out of war on a modus vivendi but FDR refused to talk with the Japanese prime minister simply because he was determined to get into war with Japan, and through that, with Germany. The American ambassador in Tokyo, Joseph Grew, knew how much the Japanese wanted to maintain peaceful relations and urged such a conference. But FDR and his fellow ardent interventionists used ruses, dodges and tricks to involve us in a totally unnecessary war. — Hamilton Fish, *FDR-The Other Side of the Coin*, Vantage Press, Inc., pages 132-134

Fish believed that Roosevelt's deception of the American people

was an immoral and infamous act. This shrewd and astute politician [Roosevelt] covered his tracks by shouting from the housetops and denouncing the attack on Pearl Harbor as a day of infamy, blaming it entirely on the Japanese.

While Roosevelt was trying to bring America into war with Japan, he was telling Americans, "While I am talking to you mothers and fathers, I give you one more assurance. *I have said this*

*before, and I shall say it again and again and
again: Your boys are not going to be sent into any
foreign wars." —* ibid. p. 29, (emphasis added).

In both cases, WWI and WWII, Wilson and
Roosevelt assured Americans that their sons would not
be going into any wars, and while they were lying, they
were preparing plans to get America to fight in the wars.
Both of these men were represented by the Jesuit-controlled press as God fearing men who would not lie.
Millions of Americans were lost in these wars. Their
blood will be on the hands of those lying, heartless politicians, and the news media, who were following their
Jesuit masters, and having no consideration for the lives
of Americans!

We have watched this same scenario played out
twice. In both Jesuit planned wars, America was brought
into war because of a terrorist attack by some foreign
power. Then, the president in office, who was looked
upon as a God-fearing man, and who was working to
bring America into the conflict, told Americans that in
order to defend freedom, we must go to war. Does this
sound familiar? Does George Bush fit this same mold?

Let us notice the emerging pattern that has been
played out several times in America.

President	Pre-Planned Terrorist Attack	War Involvement
Woodrow Wilson	The Lusitania Attack	World War I
Franklin Roosevelt	Pearl Harbor	World War II
George Bush	September 11- World Trade Center	War on Terror

Illuminist/Jesuit Albert Pike declared that the Second World War would result in an expansion of Russian influence and the creation of a state of Israel in
Palestine. Did the Second World War do those things?
Russian influence greatly increased following the Second World War. The Russian government took control

of several satellite countries including East Berlin. The Second World War also brought about the creation of the state of Israel in Palestine. The Jews were given the strip of land along the eastern shores of the Mediterranean Sea. Albert Pike is batting 1000%. Are we listening?

According to Pike, Illuminati agents would stir up the Third World War between the Zionists and the Arabs. Since the Illuminati is a front organization for the Jesuits, the Jesuits created the current war on terror. What event was it that caused the involvement of America in this conflict? It was the tragic events of September 11, 2001. Could it be that the World Trade Center attacks, just like the Lusitania and Pearl Harbor, were orchestrated to bring America into this conflict? To think anything else but this is ridiculous! None of the newscasters have said this. None of the newspapers have stated this. None of our ministers have said this. The magazines haven't declared this. Is it possible that all of these outlets are controlled by the Jesuits? If so, they naturally would not betray their hidden masters.

This conflict was to originate between the Zionists and the Arabs. Who are the Zionists? They are Jews and those who are pro-Israel. In the current war on terror, who is fighting? The Americans and the English, the two most pro-Israeli nations on the earth, are at war against the radical Arabs of Afghanistan, Iraq, and Iran. The conflict, according to Pike, was planned to extend worldwide. Soon the world would become so fed up with the horrors of war that they would welcome anything that promised peace. At that moment, the 'pure doctrine of Lucifer' would be manifested in the earth.

What is the pure doctrine of Lucifer? Lucifer was the name that was originally given to Satan in heaven. When Satan revolted against God and the government of heaven, his name was changed to Satan.

And there was war in heaven: Michael and his angels fought against the dragon; and the dragon fought and his angels, And prevailed not; neither was their place found any more in heaven. And the great dragon was cast out, that old serpent, called the Devil, and Satan, which deceiveth the whole world: he was cast out into the earth, and his angels were cast out with him. — Revelation 12:7-9.

The pure doctrine of Lucifer is Sun worship. This is the reason most people go to church and worship on the first day of the week, Sunday, the day of the sun instead of on the seventh-day of the week, Saturday, God's holy Sabbath day of the Fourth Commandment. Toward the end of the third world war, the war on terror, the whole world will be forced to worship on Satan's counterfeit day, Sunday.

Much more information on this is coming up in following chapters. Complete information is also available in the book, *When the United States Passes the National Sunday Law As Predicted in the Bible*, which can be ordered free of charge from Truth Triumphant Ministries, P. O. Box 1417, Eustis, Florida 32727, USA.

Chapter 11

THE HAND THAT STILL
INTERVENES

It may be surprising to learn that even the Bible talks about much of the subject matter we have covered so far. It has considerable information about the papacy, its associates, and what the papacy will be able to accomplish in the near future in their efforts to regain their extensive political power they enjoyed during the Dark Ages.

One of the problems people have with the Bible and especially the books of Daniel and Revelation is that it uses many symbols. This is not a problem, however, because the Bible, itself, explains what all these symbols mean. When you understand the symbols, you can read the Bible as clearly as if reading plain text. In the following discussion, all the symbols used will be made perfectly clear.

Starting with Revelation, chapter 17, and verse 1 (Usually written as Revelation 17:1) we read: "...I will show unto thee the judgment of the great whore that sitteth upon many waters." Here we have the first two symbols that we must consider: the great whore and waters. The Bible uses the symbol of a woman to represent a church. A pure woman represents God's true church, and an impure woman, a whore, as we just read, represents one of the many false or counterfeit churches.

Watch carefully as the Bible interprets itself. Isaiah 1:1,21 says, "The vision of Isaiah...which he saw concerning Judah and Jerusalem... How is the faithful city become an harlot: it was full of judgment; righteousness lodged in it; but now murderers." Jerusalem in this verse represents God's true church at that time in the Old Testament, and God said they had become a harlot because His people had fallen deep into sin.

Jeremiah says the same thing. "...Hast thou seen that which backsliding Israel hath done? She is gone up upon every high mountain and under every green tree, and there hath played the harlot." (Jeremiah 3:6). Israel, God's people, in the days of Josiah the king, had grievously departed from God's law and were worshiping the gods of the heathen around them. In their back-slidden condition, Jeremiah was impressed by God to rebuke His people; in so doing, Jeremiah said they were acting like a harlot. Here again, as in Isaiah, when God's professed people fell into sin, they were referred to as a harlot.

Ezekiel says the same thing yet again. "Son of man, cause Jerusalem to know her abominations. . . . But thou didst trust in thine own beauty, and playedst the harlot because of thy renown, and pouredst out thy fornications on every one that passed by." (Ezekiel 16:2,15). This was a very common thing in Israel. His people, His church, would forsake Him, and God used one of His prophets to call His people a harlot or a whore.

Finally, another prophet, Hosea, was asked to do a very strange thing. As an object lesson to illustrate the unfaithfulness of God's people, Hosea was told to marry Gomer, a prostitute. Hosea represented God, and Gomer represented Israel, God's people. Hosea was to marry Gomer to show God's tender, loving regard for His erring people. "...Go, take unto thee a wife of whoredoms and children of whoredoms: for the land hath committed great whoredom, departing from the Lord." (Hosea 1:2).

When speaking of prophecy, the Bible uses the symbols of a whore, harlot, and prostitute to represent a church that has forsaken God's law. Revelation 17:1 declared, "...*I will shew unto thee the judgments of the great whore* that sitteth upon many waters." This passage also declares that this apostate church sits upon many waters. Revelation 17:15 tells us, "...The waters which thou sawest, where the whore sitteth, are peoples, and multitudes, and nations, and tongues." Thus, this apostate church rose up in a heavily populated areas of the Mediterranean world. Can you think of a church in apostasy (an unfaithful church) that rose up in the Mediterranean world?

Revelation 17:2 states "With whom the kings of the earth have committed fornication and the inhabitants of the earth have been made drunk with the wine of her fornication." The kings of the earth are the leaders, the presidents, the prime ministers, and the dictators of the world. Verse two tells us that the leaders of the world are connected to this false church. Can you think of a church that has for a long time connected itself to governments and leaders? This church demands that the church and state be tied together so that she can control the leaders. This church believes that it rules all leaders by divine right, meaning that all rulers govern with the church's permission. Can you think of the church that rose up in Europe and demands control of the leaders of our world by divine right?

Revelation 18:24 gives us more information on this whore or apostate (unfaithful) church. "And in her [this apostate church] was found the blood of prophets, and of saints, and of all that were slain upon the earth." This apostate church is responsible for the blood shed in our world. Knowing that and the fact that this church controls the leaders of nations, who then is responsible for persecution, war and terrorism? The Al Quaida, the Taliban, Osama bin Ladan, Saddam Hussein? No. Revelation 17 and 18 say that the responsibility for war and terrorism lies at the door of this apostate church.

We have seen that this apostate church

1. rises in the area of Europe and the Mediterranean Sea,

2 .controls the leaders of our world,

3. has persecuted God's people and prophets, and is responsible for wars, terror attacks, and all manner of bloodshed.

This great whore of Revelation can only be the Roman Catholic Church. She alone meets all the specifications of this prophecy. Since the Bible declares that she controls the leaders of our world, and is responsible for the blood shed in our world, then —

1. Who runs the White House?
2. Who was behind September 11?
3. Who is behind the war on terror?
4. Who controls Tony Blair?
5. Who controls Saddam Hussein?
6. Who was responsible for Vietnam?
7. Who controls Fidel Castro?
8. Who is responsible for the wars of the last 15 centuries?
9. Who controls the drug trade?

A book by Dr. L. A. Lehman entitled *Behind the Dictators* has a cover picture of four leaders in Europe during World War II. Connected to each of them are strings, and a man at the top is dangling their strings, because these leaders are mere puppets. The man at the top pulling the strings is Pope Pius XII who ruled the world from 1939-1958.

According to Revelation 17

and 18, the only correct view of Vietnam is the one given by Avro Manhattan in his book, *Vietnam: Why Did We Go?* We saw in a previous chapter that Manhattan shows that the papacy and the Jesuits were the chief instigators of that war. Their intention was to gain a powerful Catholic foothold in Southeast Asia, and to crush the strong Buddhist presence in the Far East. All other reasons given for the Vietnam war are total lies.

The many books written concerning the two World Wars are correct only as they portray the role of the Catholic Church and the Jesuit Order in these conflicts. It is a gross misrepresentation of the facts to claim that Adolf Hitler, Benito Mussolini, Francisco Franco, Josef Stalin, Winston Churchill, and Franklin Roosevelt were the chief movers in that war. The Catholic Church controlled and manipulated all of these leaders.

George Bush, Dick Cheney, Colin Powell, the Taliban, Osama bin Ladan, Saddam Hussein, and others are paraded before our eyes as the key players in the war on terror. We have seen that the Bible reveals a far different scenario. All of these people are doing what they are being told to do by the Jesuits and the papacy. The current war is a religious conflict to further the papacy's design for world take over, when they will rule the world from Jerusalem. This is the only possible conclusion one can draw if we understand what the Bible tells us.

There are two other points from the chapters in Revelation we have been considering that are very important to this discussion. Revelation 18:3 says, "For all nations have drunk of the wine of the wrath of her fornication, and the kings of the earth have committed fornication with her, and *the merchants of the earth are waxed rich through the abundance of her delicacies.*" In this passage, we see another powerful entity in this world that is connected to the Jesuits and the papacy: the merchants of the earth. They are rich and powerful because they are connected to the great whore. Revelation 18:15 adds this, "*The merchants of these things, which were made rich by her*, shall stand afar off for the fear of her torment, weeping and wailing…" Who are the merchants? They are the buyers and sellers, merchandizing the commodities of earth. Revelation 18:11-13 lists some of the things that they buy and sell, "…gold, and silver, and precious stones, and of pearls, and of fine linen, and purple, and silk, and scarlet, and all thyine wood, and all manner vessels of ivory, and all manner vessels of most precious wood, and of brass, and iron, and marble, and cinnamon, and odours, and ointments, and frankincense, and wine, and oil, and fine flour, and wheat, and beasts, and sheep, and horses, and chariots, and slaves, and souls of men." That's quite a Christmas list, isn't it?

According to Revelation 17 and 18, the wealthy of the earth are made so because of their connection to the Jesuits and the papacy. The worldly rich have bowed low before the god of the Vatican and have been given rich rewards in return. We have seen several times that the granddaddy of all the world's wealthy families are the Rothschilds. We have also seen from Saussy's book, *Rulers of Evil,* pages 160, 161, that the Rothschild's hold the keys to, and are the guardians of, the Vatican's treasures. We have also seen that the Rockefellers, the Morgans, the Carnegies, the Fords, the Stanfords, and the Harrimans have all become rich through their connection to the papacy. Many more names could be added to that list. Cecil B. Rhodes and the Rhodes Scholarship, the Getty tycoons, the Onassis family, and the Kennedys can all be traced right back to the Vatican as the source of their millions.

How certain men and their families became rich overnight are fascinating stories. To show how it works, think of an American family that used to own a few little five and dime stores in Arkansas. That family has five siblings in the top ten chart of the wealthiest people in America. The family is the Waltons of Walmart and

Sam's Club fame. A little digging into the way Sam Walton went from small store owner to multi-billionaire is very shocking. The man who financed Walton in his Walmart and Sam's Club enterprises was Jackson Stephens, a multi-billionaire.

The records reveal that Stephens owns many corporations, one of which is a bank in Mena, Arkansas where billions of dollars of drug money were laundered. Stephens and an Indonesian by the name of James Riady used this bank almost exclusively for laundering the Mena-Clinton-Bush drug money that came into the Mena Airport. This money was from the guns for drugs sales that were going on between the bureaucrats in Washington and the Sandinistas of Nicaragua.

> Clinton, while governor of Arkansas, which is Rockefeller's back yard, got involved with the elite's drug running. Nella and Mena Airports in south-west Arkansas were part of the drug running system that is related to the Iran-Contra scandal. A reporter from a small newspaper in a small Arkansas town asked why Larry Nichols worked for the Arkansas Development Finance Authority. The question seems innocent enough, but the answers began to uncover the whole web of intrigue that involved the drug running and illegal arms shipments to Central America that both Bush and Clinton were involved in. — Fritz Springmeier, *Bloodlines of the Illuminati*, Ambassador House, p. 326.

Stephens has used much of this money to finance both Republican George Bush and Democrat Bill Clinton in their respective presidential campaigns. How could Stephens do such a thing? Both Bush and Clinton were working as Jesuit agents. Since Stephens also is a Jesuit agent, he could easily fund men from both parties.

Not only did Stephens use the drug money for presidential campaigns, but so much money came into Arkansas that the Attorney General and the then Governor Bill Clinton, along with Stephens and his company, began putting it into businesses that had images of being patriotic Americans. Walmart was one of many businesses that benefited. Two other companies, that came into prominence during the reign of Stephens and Clinton in Arkansas, were Hunt Trucking and Tyson Foods. Tyson foods, which has become known as the chicken king of America, even stooped so low as to stuff chickens with drugs and then send them across America. One of the board members of Walmart for years was Hillary Clinton. She also served as Walmart's chief counsel. Walmart, Tyson Foods, and Hunt Trucking were three companies that have become wealthy, corporate giants because of their unlawful and evil association with Jesuit agents who are working to destroy our Constitution and the great Protestant principles of America!

Revelation 17:5 tells us of another entity that is tied to the papacy and the Jesuits. "And upon her forehead was a name written, MYSTERY BABYLON THE GREAT, THE MOTHER OF HARLOTS AND ABOMINATIONS OF THE EARTH." The word "Babylon" means confusion. The name of the great whore, the apostate Roman Catholic Church, is called Babylon the Great because she has brought total confusion into the world, claiming to be following Christ and the Bible, while leading multitudes away from Jesus and the plain teachings of Scripture. In the process of turning people from the Bible, the church claims to be the only gateway to heaven. *The Babylon here has nothing to do with the attempted rebuilding of the ancient city of Babylon in the area of Iraq today!*

This verse indicates that the Catholic Church is the Mother church, the mother of every abominable and wicked thing that has been foisted on the world in the name of religion. We also see that the Catholic Church has many daughters who are harlots as well; for the verse says "BABYLON THE GREAT, *THE MOTHER OF HARLOTS.*" To what could these harlot daughters be referring? We have seen that the symbol of an impure woman in Scripture represents an apostate church. (Isaiah 1:21; Jeremiah 3:6; Ezekiel 16:15; Hosea). Plugging these passages back into Revelation 17, we can only arrive at the conclusion that there are other churches that are following in the papacy's footsteps. These churches can only be the ones that once broke away from the mother church, but have since that time been gradually coming back to her. The harlot daughters of the papacy represent the Protestant churches of today that are no longer protesting against Rome's abuses, but are rather finding harmony in working with her. These apostate Protestant churches of today are the Sunday-keeping harlot daughters of the mother Roman Catholic Church!

Alberto Rivera is an ex-Jesuit priest who offers some very valuable insight into the apostasy of the Protestant churches of today. He carried out many evil deeds for the Jesuit Order. However, he responded to the leading of the Holy Spirit and left the Jesuits and became a follower of the Lord, Jesus Christ. While some of his understandings of Scripture were not correct, Rivera was very clear on the role of the Jesuits and the Vatican in history. Eventually, Rivera died a martyr, having been poisoned by the Jesuits. Rivera discussed the Jesuits' desire to infiltrate and takeover all Protestant churches and lead them to follow the doctrine of the papacy. He stated that a sign would be given to Jesuits worldwide when every Protestant denomination had been successfully infiltrated and overcome by the Jesuits.

The sign was to be when a President of the U.S. took his oath of office facing an obelisk. For the first time in U.S. history, the swearing in ceremonies were moved to the West front of the

capitol, and President Ronald Reagan faced the
Washington Monument. This happened January
20, 1981. — Jack Chick, *The Godfathers*, *Alberto
Part Three*, Chick Publications, page 26.

Some may think that Alberto does not know what
he is talking about. They probably believe that their
church has not been taken over by the Jesuits. Consider
this:

1. Is your church still protesting against the
   tyranny of the papacy?

2. Does your church still teach that the papacy is
   the anti-christ, or is it something that your
   church once taught, but now shies away from
   because it is not politically correct?

3. Does your church engage in celebration style
   church services that are more contemporary
   with the times and have more upbeat music?
   This was part of the papacy's plan at Vatican
   II in taking over all the churches.

4. Is your church forgetting their historic teachings and becoming more modern, casting away
   the old truths as relics of the past?

5. Are your church periodicals finding more and
   more good things to say about the papacy,
   even considering the Vatican leaders to be fine
   Christian people?

6. Is your church willing to join the ecumenical
   movement, even if it means sacrificing some
   basic teachings or principles that the church
   once believed?

If you can answer yes to one or more of these questions, or yes to all of these questions, then Alberto Rivera
is right. Are there any major religious bodies or denomi-

nations today that don't meet these criteria?

It is interesting that Pope John Paul II agrees with Alberto Rivera. John Paul made a statement in which he declared a major concern of the Vatican. He is concerned about new religious groups that are arising in America that are warning the world about the plans of the papacy to take over the world. These new groups are telling the world that the papacy is still the antichrist, and, according to John Paul II, these groups are seriously affecting the plans of the papacy.

> The proselytizing activity of the sects and new religious groups of America is a grave hindrance to the work of evangelization.... [what he means is that there are independent religious groups that are hindering the papacy's drive to take over the world.] The success of proselytism by the sects and new religious groups in America cannot be ignored. It demands of the Church on the continent a thorough study, to be carried out in each nation and at the international level.... For the response to the challenge of the sects to be effective, there is a need for an appropriate coordination of initiatives among dioceses, aimed at bringing about a more effective cooperation through shared projects which will produce better results. — Pope John Paul II, *The Challenge of the Sects*, Exhortation, Article 73.

John Paul did not express concern about denominations that have been around for a century or two. Why? The answer is obvious; those denominations are of no concern to John Paul because they have been infiltrated and taken over by the Jesuits. Those churches have stopped protesting about the evils of the papacy! John Paul is concerned about groups that have arisen in the last few decades, who, in response to the suppression of truth in their mainline churches, have been forced to preach the truth outside of these churches.

According to Revelation 17:5, the Catholic Church has many harlot daughters. According to Alberto Rivera and John Paul II, those harlot daughters include every apostate Protestant church that has forsaken the Biblical message, and keeps Sunday instead of the Bible Sabbath! When a denomination refuses to give the straight Biblical truth, that denomination is committing spiritual adultery before God, and is considered to be a harlot.

Revelation 17 supports every principle outlined in this book. It reveals the control of the papacy's Jesuits over the leaders of our world, over the wealthy of the earth, and over the churches of today.

Chapter 12

DIVINE HAND OVER THE UNITED STATES REMOVED

The change of the Sabbath is a sign or mark of the authority of the Romish Church. Those who, understanding the claims of the fourth commandment, choose to observe the false sabbath in the place of the true, are thereby paying homage to that power by which alone it is commanded. The mark of the beast is the papal sabbath, which has been accepted by the world in the place of the day of God's appointment.

There are true Christians in every church, not excepting the Roman Catholic communion. None are condemned until they have had the light and have seen the obligation of the fourth commandment. But when the decree shall go forth enforcing the counterfeit sabbath, and the loud cry of "the third angel" shall warn men against the worship of the beast and his image, the line will be clearly drawn between the false and the true. Then those who still continue in transgression will receive the mark of the beast.

With rapid steps we are approaching this period. When Protestant churches shall unite with the secular power in sustaining a false religion, for opposing which their ancestors endured the fiercest persecution, then will the papal Sabbath be enforced by the combined authority of church and State. There will *be a national apostasy* [Apostasy is defined as the abandonment of Biblical Truths], *which will end only in national ruin.*

Marvelous in her shrewdness and cunning is the Roman Catholic Church. She presents a fair front to the world, covering with apologies her record of horrible cruelties, and declaring that her spirit of persecution no longer exists. But she is the same as in the days of the Reformation, when men of God stood up at the peril of their lives to expose her iniquity; the same as when she assumed the power to control kings and princes, and claimed the prerogatives of God. She may clothe herself in Christlike garments, the better to carry forward her purposes; but she still retains the venom of the serpent, and her principles are exerting their influence in legislative halls, in churches, and in the hearts of men. Her spirit is no less cruel and despotic now than when it crushed out human liberty, and slew the saints of the Most High.

By compromises and concessions, Protestants have tampered with and patronized popery, giving her vantage-ground which papists themselves are surprised to see and fail to understand. The Protestant world needs to be aroused to resist the advances of this most dangerous foe to civil and religious liberty.

When the State [the United States] shall enforce the decrees and sustain the institutions of the church, then will Protestant America have formed an image of the Papacy. Then the true church will be assailed by persecution as were God's people in ancient times. Almost every century furnishes instances of what human hearts, controlled by rage and malice, can do under a plea of serving God by protecting the rights of the church and State. The Protestant churches that have followed in the steps of Rome by forming alliances with worldly powers have manifested a similar desire to restrict liberty of conscience. How many non-conformist ministers have suffered under the power of the Church of England! Persecution always follows a restriction of religious liberty on the part of secular governments.—E. G. White, *The Signs of the Times*, Pacific Press, November 8, 1899. (Emphases added).

God has a law which ... is designed to govern the inhabitants of this world. Christ died that the human family might be brought back to their allegiance to God. He was their only hope of redemption. He did not suffer and die on Calvary's cross to annul the law, because he would thus be the administrator of sin by perpetuating transgression. If the law of God could have been changed, or one precept of it altered to meet man's fallen condition, then the Son of God need not have come into our world and died. But because the law of God was changeless in its character; because not one principle of it, not even a jot or a tittle, could be dishonored and swept away, God consented to let his Son take upon himself the results of man's transgression of that law, thus making it possible for man to be pardoned, and to become obedient to all God's commandments. It is the righteousness and perfection of his Son, who takes upon himself our sins, our defects, our weaknesses, which God accepts; and through faith in the merits of the blood of a crucified and risen Saviour we are prisoners of hope. Christ's righteousness becomes our righteousness, if we sustain a living connection with him. Then we cease to transgress the holy law of God, and become partakers of the divine nature.

A time is coming when the law of God is, in a special sense, to be made void in our land. The rulers of our nation will, by legislative enactments, enforce the Sunday law, and thus God's people be brought into great peril. When our nation, in its legislative councils, shall enact laws to bind the consciences of men in regard to their religious privileges, enforcing Sunday observance, and bringing oppressive power to bear against those who keep the seventh-day Sabbath [Saturday], the law of God will, to all intents and purposes, be made void in our land; and *national apostasy will be followed by national ruin.* — E.G. White, *Advent Review and Sabbath Herald, Review & Herald*, December 18, 1888. (Emphases added).

The time has come when judgment is fallen in the streets, and equity cannot enter, and he that departeth from evil maketh himself a prey.... The people of the United States have been a favored people; but when they restrict religious liberty, surrender Protestantism, and give countenance to popery, the measure of their guilt will be full, and "national apostasy" will be registered in the books of heaven. *The result of this apostasy will be national ruin.* — E.G. White, *Advent Review and Sabbath Herald, Review & Herald*, May 2, 1893. (Emphases added).

But the time to receive the mark of the beast, as designated in prophecy, has not yet come. The testing time has not yet come. There are true Christians in every church, not excepting the Roman Catholic communion. None are condemned until they have had the light and have seen the obligation of the fourth commandment. But when the decree shall go forth enforcing the counterfeit Sabbath, and when the loud cry of the third angel shall warn men against the worship of the beast and his image, the line will be clearly drawn between the false and the true. Then those who still continue in transgression will receive the mark of the beast in their foreheads or in their hands.

With rapid steps we are approaching this period. When Protestant churches shall unite with the secular power to sustain a false religion, for opposing which their ancestors endured the fiercest persecution, then will the papal Sabbath be enforced by the combined authority of church and state. *There will be a national apostasy, which will end only in national ruin.* — E.G. White, Bible Training School, *Review & Herald*, February 1, 1913. (Emphases added).

We are now making our choice, and we shall soon discern between him that serveth God and him that serveth him not. Read the fourth chapter of Malachi, and think about it seriously. The day of God is right upon us. The world has converted the church. Both are in harmony, and are acting upon a short-sighted policy. Protestants will work upon the rulers of the land to make laws to restore the lost ascendancy of the man of sin [the pope], who sits in the temple of God, showing himself that he is God. The Roman Catholic principles will be taken under the care and protection of the State. *This national apostasy will speedily be followed by national ruin.* The protest of Bible truth will be no longer tolerated by those who have made not the law of God their rule of life. Then will the voice be heard from the graves of martyrs, represented by the souls which John saw slain for the word of God and the testimony of Jesus Christ which they held; then the prayer will ascend from every true child of God, "It is time, Lord, for thee to work: for they have made void thy law." — E.G. White, *The General Conference Bulletin*, *Review & Herald*, January 1, 1900. (Emphases added).

Men are prone to abuse the long suffering of God, and to presume on his forbearance. But there is a point in human iniquity when it is time for God to interfere; and terrible are the issues. "The Lord is slow to anger, and great in power, and will not at all acquit the wicked. [Nahum 1:3]" The long-suffering of God is wonderful, because he puts constraint on his own attributes; but punishment is none the less certain. Every century of profligacy has treasured up wrath against the day of wrath; and when the time comes, and the iniquity is full, then God will do his strange work. It will be found a terrible thing to have worn out the divine patience; for the wrath of God will fall so signally and strongly that it is represented as being unmixed with mercy.... It is at the time of the national apostasy, when, acting on the policy of Satan, the rulers of the land will rank themselves on the side of the man of sin [the pope] — it is then the measure of guilt is full; *the national apostasy is the signal for national ruin.* — E.G. White, General Conference Daily Bulletin, *Review & Herald*, April 13, 1891. (Emphases added).

Already the doctrine that men are released from obedience to God's requirements has weakened the force of moral obligation, and opened the flood-gates of iniquity upon the world. Lawlessness, dissipation, and corruption are sweeping in upon us like an overwhelming tide. In the family, Satan is at work. His banner waves, even in professedly Christian households. There is envy, evil surmising, hypocrisy; estrangement, emulation, strife, betrayal of sacred trusts, indulgence of lust. The whole system of religious principles and doctrines, which should form the foundation and framework of social life, seems to be a tottering mass, ready to fall to ruin. The vilest of criminals, when thrown into prison for their offenses, are often made the recipients of gifts and attentions, as if they had attained an enviable distinction. The greatest publicity is given to their character and crimes. The papers publish the revolting details of vice, thus initiating others into the practice of fraud, robbery, and murder; and Satan exults in the success of his hellish schemes. The infatuation of vice, the wanton taking of life, the terrible increase of intemperance and iniquity of every order and degree, should arouse all who fear God to inquire what can be done to stay the tide of evil.

Courts of justice are corrupt. Rulers are actuated by desire for gain, and love of sensual pleasure. Intemperance has beclouded the faculties of many, so that Satan has almost complete control of them. Jurists are perverted, bribed, deluded. Drunkenness and revelry, passion envy, dishonesty of every sort, are represented among those who administer the laws. "Justice standeth afar off; for truth is fallen in the street, and equity cannot enter.[Isaiah 59:14]"

Our land is in jeopardy. The time is drawing on when its legislators shall so abjure the principles of Protestantism as to give countenance to Romish [Catholic] apostasy. The people for whom God has so marvelously wrought, strengthening them to throw off the galling yoke of popery, will, by a national act, give vigor to the corrupt faith of Rome, and thus arouse the tyranny which only waits for a touch to start again into cruelty and despotism. With rapid steps are we already approaching this period. When Protestant churches shall seek the support of the secular power, thus following the example of that apostate church, for opposing which their ancestors endured the fiercest persecution, then will there *be a national apostasy which will end only in national ruin.* — E.G. White, *The Signs of the Times,* Pacific Press, July 4, 1899. (Emphases added).

With rapid steps we are approaching this period. When Protestant churches shall unite with the secular power to sustain a false religion, for opposing which their ancestors endured the fiercest persecution, then will the papal sabbath [Sunday] be enforced by the combined authority of church and state. There will be a national apostasy, which will end only in national ruin. — E.G. White, *Manuscript 51,* Pacific Press, 1899.